After Further Review

A fan's guide to understanding
what's really happening on the football field

Ken Woody

MAX-EX
BOOK
PUBLISHING

ISBN-13: 978-1542350693
ISBN-10: 1542350697

 MAX-EX
BOOK
PUBLISHING

Author information:

web: coachkenwoody.com
email: coachkenwoody@gmail.com
twitter: #woody8783

Photos © 2017 by Jerry Thompson

Contents

To the three greatest coaches in my life: Jerry Frei, University of Oregon; Don Harney, Roosevelt High School; and my dad, Howard, who asked me at tough times in my life, "What are you going to do about it?"

To my current head coach and beautiful wife, Mary, who has the toughest coaching job of all, and to my daughter, Patricia, whose determination and heart easily rank with that of the best players I've ever coached. Your courage and love make this old coach very proud. I love you both!

Introduction

What's all the excitement about?

Football: A sport that bears the same relation to education that bull-fighting does to agriculture.

— **Elbert Hubbard**

It's a brilliant fall day, bedazzled by the reds and oranges of falling leaves and the drumbeats of the marching bands, stirring the spirited hopes of millions of football fans across the country. There are pep rallies and tailgate food and drink fests that bring together old friends and rivals for the autumn ritual that is football in America. Across the country, crowds pack stadiums, shoulder to shoulder, to cheer on the players who act out the gridiron's compelling dramas. The referee blows the whistle. A player boots the ball. The fans roar in anticipation of the game that's about to unfold.

There's just one slight problem: A large number of those fans have no clue what's going on in front of them — what's *really* going on, like the newbie who asked, "If it rains, do all the players wear long pants?"

For the average spectator, enjoying the game and understanding it are two different things. It's easy to be carried away by the passion of football and still not have a sense of what's happening on the field. To those fans, only a glance at the scoreboard gives meaning to the chaos whirling in front of them.

The aim of this book is to help you learn to watch more than the collisions and pileups around the football. Those are exciting, but will resonate more when you have context. Most fans lack the knowledge to fully enjoy the game, and most books about watching football can be too technical or boring, aimed at readers who already have an understanding based on playing or coaching. Whether you're new to this wonderful game, a novice seeking to know more or a veteran fan who wants to know more, this book will provide you with a deeper understanding of the nuances and strategy behind the jarring tackles, long runs and amazing pass plays. This book is for those who are embarrassed to ask questions and are frustrated watching something they don't understand.

It covers the fundamentals for players and fine points for the coaches; how the different positions relate to each other; how players perform in the variety of formations; and philosophies coaches employ. You're going to learn why certain things happen in a football game and where to look to see them happen.

You'll note some redundancy in the book; key details are repeated at various points to reinforce your understanding. That's what good coaching is all about.

As you read this book, you'll learn through insights I've gleaned from a 55-year involvement in football as a player, Division I college coach, television commentator and football columnist for *The* (Eugene, Oregon) *Register-Guard* newspaper, which covers one of the country's winningest programs since 2010, the University of Oregon. And you'll learn from someone who's also been a teacher and administrator — who not only understands his subject but the learning process in general.

In my 18-year career as a college football coach, I spent 13 of those seasons in the press box, high above the field with the best view of the action and a direct line to coaches and players on the sidelines. In my first year of coaching at Oregon, where I'd played as a receiver, defensive back and place kicker, I sat next to my mentor, John Robinson, who was the coordinator of an offense that featured future All-Pro Hall of Famers Dan Fouts and Bobby Moore (Ahmad Rashad).

Coach Robinson, who would go on to be head coach at USC, the Los Angeles Rams and the University of Nevada Las Vegas, was a brilliant, innovative coach and teacher. He connected deeply with his players and injected fun and humor into his approach.

"Woody," he once told me, "you're going to be a good coach because you're a pain in the ass." My job was to give Coach Robinson the down, first-down distance and field position after each play so he'd know the right call for the next one.

Robinson's instructions were to "watch the free safety every play; never mind about the ball." This was difficult, because the natural inclination is to watch the ball; after all, that's where the action is, or seems to be. After several "ass chewings" for watching the ball, I became more skilled at watching the diverse elements of the game. I began to see how much more was going on than a pile of players around the ball. The average fan misses the individual battles on the line of scrimmage and the synergy of the divergent players working as a single unit, because they don't know where or when to look.

"Leaders aren't born, they are made. And they are made just like anything else, through hard work. And that's the price we'll have to pay to achieve that goal or any goal."
— **Vince Lombardi, coach, Green Bay Packers**

I have watched thousands of hours of game film over the years, repeatedly, in slow motion; perhaps one play more than two dozen times, looking at what each individual player on offense and defense did. This widened my — no pun intended — field of vision; I could see more of the game, without watching the ball. I began to recognize the secondary elements of the game that made the difference between winning and losing.

As for Coach "Robby's" directive, I learned that if the free safety was playing in the middle of the field, the pass coverage was either man-to-man or three-deep zone and the offense could count on the split end being open on a sideline pass pattern. But, if the free safety lined up on the hash mark instead of the middle, and the strong safety was in the same position across the field, it was a different defense and the split end would be covered. Such is the chess match that, play after play, goes on between competing coaches.

My coaching career progressed and, at 26, I became head coach at Whitman College. I learned many lessons from film study, and also the hard way: during the game, as it happened on the field. I learned that you can't have your outside linebacker in an "eagle" position (lined up over the offensive tackle) and rush the passer. The quarterback eluded the rush and scrambled to the side where I should have had the linebacker line up, and ran for a 65-yard touchdown. It cost us six points, a lesson learned the hard way, but never forgotten.

Much of my learning came as a player. In my first Pee Wee tackle football game at age 12, I was on the kickoff team (end man on the left side), charged with running straight down the field and containing the kickoff returner, forcing him to turn toward the rest of our team. It was my first play ever, and I was so excited I totally forgot my responsibility. I chased the returner away from me and then he handed the ball to a teammate reversing the field back toward me, and based on my over commitment, around me, for a 75-yard touchdown. I was never fooled by a reverse play again in my 12-year playing career — despite there being many times when I faced the same situation.

The book is divided into chapters, covering a football game as it unfolds for the fan: taking your seat, cheering the action on the field; and the inevitable second-guessing that comes after each play and each game. Care has been taken to avoid piling up too much detail at a time and mixing in information from both the coaches' and players' perspective. You will read about what constitutes "good coaching" and "good playing" as well as "gamebreakers" for both — and for you, the fan. Football in America has a long and storied history, and so I've added snippets about its past to increase your reading pleasure and perspective.

For me, there are few things more enjoyable than talking ball with other coaches and fans, especially those who ask questions and have a desire to learn. The game is fascinating and the conversations more invigorating than talking politics, although both subjects involve some rough stuff. We may never understand the political world, but we can make sense out of football and experience why the game fires the soul. Enjoy the book, and remember to "watch the free safety."

1.

Pre-game: Field and Scoring

Football is not a game but a religion, a metaphysical island of fundamental truth in a highly verbalized disguised society, a throwback of 30,000 generations of anthropological time.

— **Arnold Mandell**

In early football, the playing fields were grass, dirt, mud or a combination of all three. In the late 1960s, artificial turf made of synthetic plastic materials — atop rubber padding — was introduced in stadiums located in climates whose playing fields were muddied by rain or snow. As time went on, artificial turf proved cost effective and held up well under heavy use by football and other sports teams. Today 65% of college football fields are artificial turf, which is easier and less expensive to maintain than grass. While early artificial fields could be as hard as parking lots, today's variety offer better impact resistance than natural grass.

One disadvantage of artificial turf is that it absorbs heat and can create serious issues for athletes in terms of respiration and hydration during hot-weather games. In addition, ask any player who's slid across a hot artificial turf and you'll find "rug burns" are a painful byproduct of playing on such fields in those conditions. Grass stains are much easier for players to bear than blood stains.

Gridiron Tradition — Indoor Football

The first indoor football game was played in 1891, matching the Springfield Training School against players from Yale in the old Madison Square Garden. The game wasn't considered successful because, according to *Football Thru the Years,* "the Garden was neither of sufficient size to accommodate a full size field nor to allow proper handling of punts." In 1934, the first successful indoor game was played in the mammoth Atlantic City Auditorium; it matched Lafayette against Washington and Jefferson. Steam rollers prepared the playing surface the night before the game while players, as they practiced, "… picked up pieces of glass and bottle tops. Reports of the game reveal that the playing surface was free of all debris and exceptionally fast."

Night Games

The first night football game was played between the University of Arizona and St. Vincents College in Los Angeles on November 25, 1905. The lights must have got in the eyes of the Wildcats as St. Vincents romped over them 55-0. Nowadays, night games are for the convenience of television and the almighty dollar. If you're a fan, a game on Thursday night might be a treat, but to the player with a chemistry final on Friday morning or the out-of-town fan, not so much.

Big Crowds

In 1925, 125,000 spectators, one of the largest crowds to ever watch a college football game, crowded Chicago's Soldiers Field to watch Army-Navy play on the day that field was dedicated. The Super Bowl, the championship game of the National Football League, annually draws the greatest world-wide television audience of any other sporting event. Tickets to see the 2017 game in person averaged $4,744; tens of thousands of fans were willing to pay such prices. Ironically, and sadly, Super Bowl Sunday shows a spike in the number of domestic disturbances reported nationally, which may speak to alcohol, the angry fans whose favorite teams have lost, and the emotional nature of the game.

The Playing Field

A football field is 100 yards long and 53⅓ yards wide with a 10-yard end zone at the end of each goal line (Diagram 1). The ball is put

Understanding the playing field

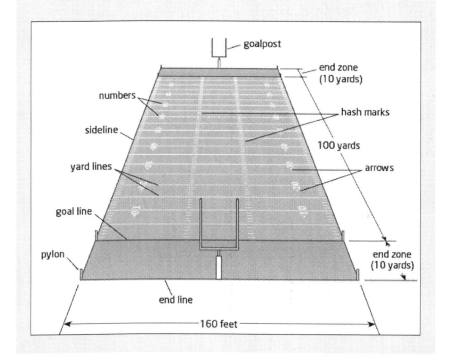

Diagram 1. The field.

into play on the hash marks, or anywhere in between, which are the markers running the length of the field 60 feet in from each sideline, creating a rough middle to the field that's 40 feet wide.

There are yard lines marked width-wise every five yards the length of the field, with the hash marks marked every yard. These lines were all created for tracking offensive progress, in particular to show how far a team needs to go to make a first down or touchdown.

The sidelines are marked from each 25-yard line to the other with a wide, white marking, denoting the player-coach box. Only eligible players, coaches and authorized equipment and medical personnel may be in those areas during play.

Such people are to stay three yards back from the field to make it easier for referees and fans to see the sideline markers and to keep unauthorized personnel out of the playing area. Examples of "unauthorized personnel" might be movie stars who support the team, wealthy alumni, girl friends and other family members.

Gridiron Tradition

The word "gridiron" described the football fields in the early 1900s, marked in a checkerboard, or grid, pattern, resembling a gridiron — a metal grid for cooking food over a fire. In 1911, a sportswriter for *Outdoor Sports and Games*, Claude H. Miller, established the term "gridiron" to the relatively new sport, writing, "The lines on a football field make a checkerboard effect and give to the field the name of 'gridiron.'" The lines were originally laid down in chalk, a cumbersome task. With artificial turf, the markings are woven into the synthetic surface and can be permanent. A team will still touch up those lines with paint at the beginning of each season.

> *"If a man watches three football games in a row, he should be declared legally dead."*
> — **Erma Bombeck, columnist**

Over time, teams have used the center of the field and their end zones to feature their mascot, nickname or sponsors in chalk or paint. In times before artificial turf, many teams laid down interesting and artistic chalk displays in their end zones, but that custom has gone by the wayside. Today, the University of Tennessee's end zones remain the most distinctive — orange-and-white checkerboard, similar to what Oregon State used in the 1960s, though the Beavers went with simply white-chalk squares interspersed by grass squares.

"How do you score points in a football game?"

When the ball is caught or carried into the opposing team's end zone — or a defensive team recovers a fumble or blocked punt in the end zone — the team doing so is awarded a touchdown, worth six points. That team is then given an "extra point" (PAT or "point-after-try") opportunity: one point by a kick through the uprights (from 3-yard-line for college and 15-yard-line for pros) or two points by a successful run or pass play (from 3-yard-line for college and 2-yard-line for pros). On a regular scrimmage play — not after a touchdown — if a ball is kicked through the uprights of the goal posts centered on the back line of the opponents' end zone, the team doing so earns a field goal, worth three points.

If a player with the ball is tackled or falls down in his team's end zone, the defensive team is awarded a safety, worth two points. Same story if a punt is blocked and goes through the end zone.

"How long is a college football game?"

The game is 60-minutes long, divided into two halves of 30 minutes and four quarters of 15 minutes. There is a 20-minute halftime period that's usually filled with marching bands, commercial announcements and recognition of key personalities and celebrations of the home school. When the referee (in the white hat) blows his whistle and makes a circle signal with his arm, the clock will start for play.

In college, the offensive team has a limit of 40 seconds to initiate each play based on the circumstance and once started, the clock will continue to run until the ball goes out of bounds, is passed incomplete or the referee calls a penalty, in which case it stops until the next play is run.

When the ball is dead (out of play), the clock will begin a new 40-second count to give officials and teams time to prepare for the next play. If the 40-second count goes past 25 — and with an injured player still down — the clock will stop.

Once the injured player is off the field, the referee will start the 25-second clock. The offense will always have at least 25 seconds between plays, unless the ball becomes dead, in which case it will have 40.

Spectators can tell how much time is remaining by looking at the game clock, but the official time is kept on the field by one of the — as they're affectionally called — "zebras." With the advent of instant-replay technology in the press box, officials often have assistance from separate official crews in the box for problems or discrepancies in the official playing time.

"What about timeouts?"

Each team is granted three timeouts per half and most coaches save them as long as possible in case they need to stop the clock towards the end of either half to make offensive or defensive adjustments in do-or-die situations or to set up for a field goal.

If the game is tied at the end of regulation time, an overtime period is played until there is a winner, with each team getting one timeout per period played. Many a game has been won or lost by the manner in which the coaches utilized, or wasted, their timeouts.

"How do overtime situations work?"

In college ball, no game can end in a tie. If knotted in regulation, the two teams play overtime periods, beginning at their opponent's 25 yard-line, until there is a winner.

Prior to the "OT," captains meet at mid-field for a second coin toss, with the winner getting to choose whether to go on offense or defense first. Most captains choose defense because their team will then know, after its opponent's offensive attempt, how many points they need to win or tie. Conversely, the team that goes on offense first lacks that perspective; does it dare settle for a field goal, knowing it can lose if its opponent scores a touchdown?

Whoever loses the coin flip gets to choose the end of the field where play will begin, its captain usually basing his choice on where friendly fans might be located or which way the wind is blowing.

Each team gets one possession that ends either in a score, a failure to get a first down or a turnover. If a team scores a touchdown, it's afforded the same PAT options as in regulation play — a one-point kick or a two-point run or pass.

If the score is still knotted after each team's attempt, a second overtime is held, the teams change ends of the field and change which team goes on offense first; thus, in the second OT, the team that was on defense first in Round I starts on offense. This process repeats — by the way, one timeout per team per OT period — until a winner is decided.

The lone derivation is that, beginning with the third OT period, a team scoring a touchdown must go for a two-point conversion, which means no more of the TD-and-kick rhythm that often prolongs ties.

In overtimes, physical conditioning is extremely important because the extra periods take their toll on energy and focus.

Beyond a turnover or a key player blowing out his knee, perhaps the worst thing that can happen to an offensive team in OT is its quarterback getting sacked on a first-play passing attempt. Given the 25-yard-line start, the lost yardage all but wipes out a chance for a field goal and puts pressure on the team to simply get a first down and maintain possession. Meanwhile, the players know if they don't score, a simple field goal can beat them.

Coaching Points

Some coaches have difficulty staying off the playing field during the game. They often argue with, or point out discrepancies to, officials. It's against the rules to do that, but referees need to make themselves available to the head coach for explanations on rulings and penalties. Otherwise, officials invite the chaos that can result from a frustrated coach not getting information he is entitled to. Some coaches are given too much freedom, which creates problems with crowd and player control along the sidelines. Players will also tell you that when their coach argues about a past play with the officials, it disrupts the team's focus for the upcoming play.

Watch the coaches on the sidelines, especially when the game gets tense. Those teams who have highly demonstrative coaches — say, going on the field to confront officials or tearing up sideline markers — often play the same way: emotional and undisciplined. Can you tell if the coaches you are observing are modeling respectful and disciplined behavior for their team? Great coaches realize the relationship between disciplined conduct on the sidelines and disciplined play on the field.

"How many coaches does a football team have?"

High school teams may have two or three full-time coaches and several part-time or volunteer coaches; the number is often dependent on ex-players or coaches who live in the school's community. Small college teams may have four or five full-time coaches and up to six more part-time and volunteers, all who would have college playing or coaching experience.

Major college teams are restricted by rule to have no more than 10-full time coaches but may have others — graduate assistants or "quality control" specialists — help. Most Division IA teams have 10-15 coaches. Pros will have 16 or more, which allows for specialization by player's position.

Beyond a head coach, a typical Division 1A college team will have an offensive coordinator who oversees the rest of the offensive staff: line coach, running backs coach, quarterback coach and receivers coach. The offensive coordinator often is the quarterback coach. Teams may split responsibilities with two line coaches or two receiver coaches for passing teams.

Defensively, there is a coordinator who also coaches, or co-coaches a position and oversees a staff that has a defensive backfield coach, a defensive line coach and linebacker coach.

As with the offense there could be split responsibilities such as two defensive back coaches, defensive line or linebacker coaches — it depends on the emphasis the head coach wants to put on those positions.

In addition, every team has a special teams coach who is responsible for organizing the kicking game. However, because there are so many players involved in special teams, several — or all of — the assistants will assist.

You would be shocked at the number of administrative personnel who support a major college football program. The University of Washington has 33 individuals who are dedicated to the Husky program. Besides 10 full-time coaches, there are graduate assistant coaches, program coordinators; quality control directors; five strength and conditioning coaches; a director of video production; a manager of football graphic design; and — I'm not making this up — an assistant director of football technology. Not to mention player personnel directors, academic coordinators, film and video specialists, nutritionists, trainers and —whew—doctors.

You can imagine what the personnel budget might be and why winning is so important to sustaining a structure like this.

Gridiron Tradition

Bo Schembechler, the late, great head coach at Michigan, was once penalized for shouting, "Ref, you stink!" from the sideline. The official promptly threw his flag, indicating a personal foul, and marched off a 15- yard penalty. As he put the ball down on the new spot, he turned and yelled back to the boiling Schembechler, "How do I smell from here?"

2.

Players' Equipment

The reason women don't play football is because 11 of them would never wear the same outfit in public.

— **Phyllis Diller, comedienne**

There's great concern about the safety of football players who play a game where tough, physical athletes generate speed and momentum and crash into each other. Concussions demand most of the spotlight at present, but there are many other injuries common to the game: torn knee ligaments, separated shoulders, ankle injuries and hand and arm damage.

Helmets

All players are required to wear protective equipment, starting with a helmet that is made of lightweight, high-impact carbon fiber and Kevlar, a synthetic fiber used in tires and protective gear — material designed to spread and dissipate the force of collisions.

In the 1890s, before helmets, players would grow their hair long, hoping to protect their head although most of the contact came with collisions and blows by the shoulder. Early improvements from "hair helmets" were designed by harness makers who put together leather straps and belts to surround the skull. These were unwieldy and led to leather headgear that looked like the helmets aviators would wear while dogfighting over France. Braving the mass momentum offensive plays of the early 1900s, dizzy defenders began asking for more padding.

Along with more padding added inside, suspension systems to cradle the skull away from the shell of the helmet were designed and, in 1940, a single-molded shell was designed by the Riddell Company, a leading helmet manufacturer today. Helmets were colorfully painted to show a team's spirit and help quarterbacks spot pass receivers down field and today are used as trademarks of the team wearing them.

> *"I have contempt for a game in which players have to wear so much equipment. Men play basketball in their underwear, which seems just right to me."*
> — Anna Quindlen, columnist

Helmets are expensive — up to $400 — and because of the dangers of top-speed collisions, players who have not been coached properly or who are disregarding the rules incur catastrophic, sometimes-permanent, injuries that lead to huge financial vulnerability to all parties concerned.

One situation shocked the sports world in 1978 when Oakland Raider defensive back Jack Tatum blasted New England's unsuspecting receiver Darryl Stingley as he was reaching for a pass thrown across the middle of the field. Stingley was paralyzed for life and died in 2007. Ironically, Tatum, who never spoke to Stingley after the accident, died in 2010.

Face Masks

All helmets are fit with a face mask that is designed to protect the eyes and nose. Face masks tend to get larger and more elaborate based on the positions players play. Offensive and defensive linemen, who battle on the line of scrimmage every play, have larger masks that cover more of the face and throat, often with a bar running vertically down the middle. But given the rugged busted mugs of some ex-linemen, the larger masks don't always do the trick, either.

There are plenty of stories over the years of fingers poking eyes or — on rare occasions — players even biting the opponent; hence, the need for more protection for players who toil in what's basically a free-for-all.

The masks of defensive backs and ball handlers on offense offer less coverage than those of linemen because a wider range of vision is more important to them. Ball carriers still complain of poking and biting in those big pileups, but an unspoken code seems to keep those stories out of the media. Today, many players wear a plastic see-through shield with their face mask for extra protection.

Sometimes you see a kicker with a single bar face mask; that's not much protection, but then again, most kickers manage to avoid body contact and feel they don't need it. Those who do wear single-bar masks hear plenty of harassment from their opponents and even teammates, who consider it wimpy and a reminder of how removed kickers are from the physical nature of the game. There's a reason kickers are the most rested, happy and healthy players on the team.

Shoulder Pads

Shoulder pads were originally made of leather and rested on top of the shoulders. In the old days, most of the body contact in the game was the result of a player using his shoulder to block or tackle an opponent. Leather gave way to plastic fiberglass pads that fit under a game jersey. They made the player look much bigger and more foreboding than he actually was. Players liked this impression, but complained about the big pads restricting their arms when they had to raise them.

In today's game, the shoulder pads are lightweight, sleek, and made of space-age composites that absorb and distribute impacts over a larger area. These materials are also used in body armor for soldiers and police officers. You can pretty much tell the position a player plays by the size of his shoulder pads. Linemen wear the biggest, while backs and kicking specialists wear the smallest. Quarterbacks, susceptible to hard, blindside tackles while passing the ball, often wear rib pads to protect from unexpected hits.

Football Pants

Football pants in the old days might be made of leather or canvas and called "mole skins." As time went by, internal pockets were built in to hold padding to protect the hips, knees and thighs. Today, players wear lightweight hip pad girdles and have fiber thigh and kneepads in synthetic pants; everything is designed for speed and efficient dispersion of built-up body heat. Light-weight pants — more like tight cycling shorts — accent the derriere of trim, skilled players but don't do so much for the backsides of those heavier fellows who play offensive or defensive line. Some players whose playing position depends on speed and agility will not wear some pads in an effort to be faster. This is not always a smart move, as severe bruises can result from hits to parts of the body that are not protected.

The rules require all players to wear helmets, hip pads, knee pads, mouthpieces, shoulder pads, socks, thigh guards, jerseys and pants. Officials do not always enforce the rule on requiring knee or hip pads.

Shoes

A player's shoes are one of the most important pieces of equipment he wears. All players want shoes that are lightweight; today's products fit that bill nicely. In the early days of football, players wore heavy shoes or boots that came above the ankle. On a muddy field, a player's shoes absorbed water and mud, which made running a more strenuous activity than it is today. Late in a game, a weary player often felt "heavy legged" because his shoes were water-logged. Today, because the mud and grass of traditional football fields have largely gone by the wayside, shoes don't accumulate mud and remain lightweight throughout the game.

Cleating can be crucial as game conditions, particularly in rain and ice, often put the team wearing regular shoes at a disadvantage. Most teams have an equipment staff that offers players a variety of options with shoes and the kinds and sizes of cleats to handle artificial turf, grass fields and all kinds of weather.

Stories abound of teams that came to play without shoe options and lost to teams that did. In 1985, Washington State's equipment manager borrowed special shoes designed for slippery conditions from the NFL Seattle Seahawks in preparation for their rival game with Washington. Every skill player had a pair while the Huskies struggled with their regular footwear. It must have made a difference as the underdog Cougars knocked off Washington on an icy field in Seattle, 21-20.

Accessories

As football became more fashionable with the public, so did the desire of individual players to put a bit of extra gear on to look stylish or rugged. To be stylish, you could go with taping your wrists or wearing white or colored compression wraps on your arms to look tough. One coach told his players "you can look tough without taping your hands, arms and elbows," and they proved it, even in freezing weather. Coaches who wanted to show their players they were "hip" stood back as the players customized for maximum effect. Eye black, originally used to cut the glare of sun in the eyes, is now used in night games, indoor games and as war paint on the whole face. Some players like to tape their ankles outside of their shoe instead of on their skin — it makes them look faster — while others wear curious rubber bands around their biceps that help guys with small arms look bigger.

The Ball

College footballs conform to the exact dimensions set down by the NCAA: 10.5 to 11.5 inches in length, with a circumference of roughly 28 inches on the long side of the ball and 21 inches on the short side, weighing between 14 and 15 ounces. The main distinction between official college footballs and those used in the NFL is two 1-inch white stripes located 3 to 3¼ inches from either end of the ball in the college game.

For each game, schools supply the referees with six footballs to be used when their team is on offense. The week before the game, teams will lightly use the balls and rub them down so they're not as slick as when they come out of the box.

"What requirements are there for assigning jersey numbers?"

Football rules require that all offensive linemen (centers, guards, tackles) wear numbers between 50 and 79, primarily so referees can keep track of eligible and ineligible pass receivers on pass plays. Offensive linemen are not eligible to catch a forward pass unless it first bounces off a defensive player.

Offensive backs and receivers must wear numbers from 1-49 and 80-99, while defensive players can wear any number. No jersey may be numbered 0. With large squads, two players may wear the same number although rules prevent both being on the field at the same time.

Coaching Points

Although rules require players to wear kneepads in their pants, many don't — and some suffer injuries because of it. In practice, coaches have their quarterbacks wear a bright-colored jersey, usually red, that warns that this player — most often a quarterback or injured player — isn't to be hit.

The rules of football prohibit a player from using his helmet as a weapon to block or tackle an opponent. Doing so puts both players at risk. Coaches have had to teach new methods of tackling because players used to be coached to keep their head and eyes up and use their helmet and face mask as the initial point of contact on a ball carrier. The idea was to stand the runner up, destroy his momentum and hold him until fellow defenders arrived and "cleaned up" with a "gang tackle."

Today's technique is to have your head up, but at the side of the ball carrier, initiating contact with the shoulder while wrapping the arms around and rolling the ball carrier to the ground. In this way, tackling has reverted back to the original method the game used in the late 1800s — and the method rugby players have always used.

Gridiron Tradition

Through the years, players and coaches have extolled the virtues of tough, physical football. In the late 1800s, players wore a minimum of equipment besides jerseys and socks. Most players wore their hair long and shaggy, like rugby players do today, in an effort to protect their heads. It wasn't until 1939 that helmets were required for all players.

As players began to get faster, stronger, bigger and more aggressive, protective equipment became a necessity and no longer carried the stigma of weakness for those who wore such protective gear. As for all the accessories, because players get so much TV "face time" and the game draws so many fans, their desire to personalize their appearance above the uniformity of the team has grown to the point where many coaches think it's a distraction. Then again, if the over-accessorized players are spearheading their teams to victory, it's hard for a coach to complain too much.

3.

The Coin Toss

In football, as in life, you must learn to play within the rules of the game.

— Hayden Fry, coach, Iowa

It's game day. The stadium is packed, the fans fortified by tailgate parties and alumni memories. The marching band is playing, the cheerleaders dancing, the hot-dog hawkers hawking. Then, at midfield, comes the first cantata in the football symphony: the coin toss.

Each team designates one or more players to represent it as captains for the ceremonial coin toss by the head official. In the old days, that was as large as the group got — an official and two players. But that's changed as public relations become more a part of the game. Now, the official and players are often accompanied by a politician if it's an election year or by a celebrity if it's the Super Bowl.

"Who chooses the captains?"

Captains are chosen by coaches, or voted on by the team, for the entire season or a single game. They're chosen for their dedication and performance. Frequently, out-of-state players may be chosen when the team plays in their home area, for reward or motivation.

"What does the referee do?"

The referee asks the visiting captain to call the toss "heads or tails." Whichever team wins the toss has the choice of receiving the kick-off, kicking off, defending one end of the field, or "deferring," which means that team will make its choice at the beginning of the second half and the other team will choose now.

"Why would a team defer its choice?"

For a couple of reasons. First, because they think they may get two consecutive possessions: the last of the first half and the first of the second half. Second, to have the option of receiving, kicking or defending the desired end of the field for the second half when it will have more knowledge of how their team is playing and the status of the game itself.

A team might not always choose to receive the kickoff. If the weather — usually wind — might be a factor, a coach might want to put the other team in a field-position hole and force it to punt against the wind when his team gets a "stop."

Another reason to choose the wind would be when a team has a dominating defense and the coach wants to show his opponent, early on, "who's the boss." Both choices are based on defense and gaining prime field position.

"Who gets to make the decision after winning the coin toss?"

The coach instructs his captains on what call to make — it's never left up to the players. A coach will instruct his captain to choose to re-ceive the kickoff if he has confidence in his offense and wants to begin the game with an aggressive plan.

If that's the case, his team will be required to kick off to begin the second half. A coach might also elect to kick off with the wind at his back because he has confidence in his defense and expects it to hold the offense to minimum yardage on its first possession, force a punt and take control of the ball with good field position.

Even though a team elects to kick off to begin the first half, it will still be the choice of the other team to kick or receive in the second

Jerry Thompson

You can't tell from the stands, but the mood of the captains at midfield is dead-serious.

half, giving it successive kickoff returns to begin both the first and second halves of the game.

This is unusual, because in this era of high-powered offenses, most teams are reluctant to give up an opportunity of going on offense and affording another offensive opportunity for their opponent. However, in 2015, before a UCLA-Texas game, the Bruins deferred and the Longhorns' captain inexplicably chose to kick off, meaning UCLA got to receive kickoffs at the start of each half — and the Texas captain, presumably, got a tongue-lashing he'll never forget.

"What goes through a coach's mind when deciding what to do?"

Playing on the road against a fired-up opponent whose crowd is going to make a lot of noise, a coach might consider this: either (a) kick off and try to hold off a hyped-up offensive team or (b) receive the kick and try to move the ball with an offense that might be nervous and jittery and need some time to settle down. It can be a difficult decision.

If the team that wins the coin toss elects to defer to the second half, it has the same choices that were available at the beginning of the game. Most teams will elect to receive unless they have a huge advantage with their defense or the prevailing weather (usually wind).

Coaching Point

It's a big mistake to win the toss and tell the referee you want to "kick off," even if that's what you — Team A — want. Why? Because the team that lost the toss — Team B — will then take the wind, not having to pick "receive" because that's automatic when Team A chooses to kick off. In this scenario, the team that won the toss — Team A — has just made a bad mistake: kicking off into the wind. The right choice would be to take the wind, in which case the other team, not wanting to kick into the wind, would pick "receive," which is just what Team A wanted in the first place: to kick off with the wind.

Gridiron Tradition

Back when there were two professional football leagues, the American Football League's 1962 playoff game featured the Houston Oilers and the Dallas Texans. The contest went into sudden death overtime. In such cases, there was another coin toss before overtime and the visiting team's captain, Abner Haynes, was not well prepared by his coach to explain his team's choice if they won the toss. He won the toss and misspoke, electing to kick off. The other team chose the wind and Haynes's team ended up kicking off into the wind, a terrible choice, especially since the game was going to be decided in sudden death, by the first team to score. Fortunately for Haynes, his team, Dallas, escaped an early exit and won in double overtime.

Army-Navy Tradition

In the Army-Navy game, both academies exchange "prisoners" at midfield before the coin toss. The "prisoners" are volunteer captive cadets and midshipman who spend the week before the game as exchange students on the opposing school's campus. The tradition is another positive aspect of the life-long rivalry that each school cherishes. Important guests such as the president of the United States, vice-president or other high-ranking cabinet members are introduced and escorted to the cheering section of the designated academy before the game. At halftime, the honored guest is escorted across the field to the other academy's section for the second half, honoring both schools in what many believe to be college football's greatest annual game.

4.

The Kickoff

Football is, after all, a wonderful way to get rid of your aggression without going to jail for it.

— **Heywood Hale Broun, commentator**

A football game starts with a kickoff. Everyone in the stadium has a nervous feeling — players, coaches and spectators alike. This is it, a game that may have been anticipated for days or even months before. As the kicker signals his readiness, the referee blows his whistle and the crowd roars in unison. The kicker and his fellow players sprint forward; the game has begun.

Before 2012, the kicking team put the ball into play from its own 40-yard line, but with the development of stronger kickers consistently driving the ball into the end zone, the kickoff was moved back to the 35-yard line to promote more kickoff returns.

One of the most boring plays in a football game is a kickoff caught in the end zone and "downed" by the would-be returner. The offense then starts from its own 25-yard line, statistically, a better spot to start than where the returner would probably reach.

There are a variety of kick formations and the kicker has a choice of any spot on the 35-yard line between the hash marks (the vertical marker dividing every five-yard distance from goal line to goal line).

It's common for a team to kick off from the hash mark and kick the ball into that corner of the field, shrinking, in effect, the area the return team has to set up its return and the area the kicking team needs to defend. Look for players switching positions just before the kick to confuse the blockers' individual blocking assignments.

"Are there different kinds of kickoffs?"

Yes. There are kickoffs after every score: touchdown, field goal or safety. After a safety the kicking team has the option of punting or place kicking. The latter is usually the choice only after a team gives up a safety and has to kick off from its own 20-yard line.

Because the kicking team has given up 15 yards of field position from the normal kickoff spot, a coach usually has his team punt because the ball can be kicked higher than a place kick, which allows the coverage team more time to get down field.

"I've found that prayers work best when you have big players."
— Knute Rockne, coach, Notre Dame

Normally, a place-kicked kickoff will go farther than a punt and is the choice by coaches for standard kickoffs.

Watch how the kickoff team — playing defense — covers its kick. You will see players in a front wave running as fast as they can to avoid blockers and to converge on the return man. There will be a secondary wave of two or three players who mirror the return man and serve as safeties, tacklers who are the last resort if the front wave fails to tackle the return man who has the ball.

Usually, the kicker is in the last wave — well, last *ripple* — and because he is not a full-time player at a defensive position, rates as a poor bet to make the tackle. Sometimes the best a kicker can do is to force the return man to alter his path inward to where regular defenders — experienced tacklers — might be able to make a last-gasp play.

Watch the kicker cover his kick and see how effective he is at avoiding blockers and "staying alive" in the play; it can be quite entertaining, even if it sometimes has a certain David-vs.-Goliath look to it.

"How do you choose your kickoff team?"

The kicker, obviously, is chosen for how far he can kick the ball, how long his kicks are in the air ("hang time") and how accurate he is at putting the ball where the coaches want it — say, far from where a great kick returner is waiting. The coverage players are usually fast, physical and good tacklers; most are defensive players who are well versed in tackling and maintaining leverage on a ball carrier.

"What's an onside kickoff?"

A team that's desperate to regain possession of the ball after scoring late in the game — or that's sensing an unsuspecting or lazy opponent earlier than that — may try an onside kick. The kick must go a minimum of 10 yards but, once it does, the football belongs to whichever team pounces on it first. If the kick doesn't go the minimum 10 yards, the kick-return team is awarded the ball wherever it is downed or blown dead, which, of course, means great "field position."

"What is a squib kick"?

A squib kick is when the ball is placed flat or at an acute angle on the kicking tee, resulting in a "knuckleball effect." Although limited in distance, a squib kick is difficult to judge and catch. Often the return team falls on the ball to prevent a fumble because the unpredictable nature of the kick prevents an organized blocking return.

Coaching Points

To cover a kick, coaches divide the width of the field into equal-sized "lanes" (Diagram 2) and the players covering are assigned one in particular. A player covering a kick should stay in his lane, and if he moves out of it to avoid a block, should move to get back into that lane; otherwise, the return team has just been gifted with a wider hole in the defense for the return man.

A covering player should never "follow the same color" jersey; that would mean two players are covering the same lane, again opening a hole in the coverage. If a covering player sees the same color jersey in front of him, he needs to find the unattended lane and change his course to cover that open lane.

Now and then, resist the temptation to watch the ball on the kickoff; instead, check the coverage and see how the return team is attempting to

The Kickoff
Key for kicking team: players stay in own lanes

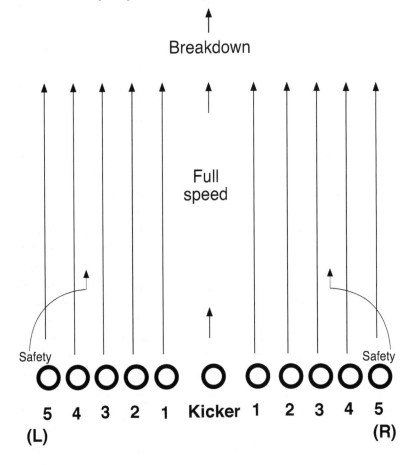

1. Stay in your lane.
2. Don't run around blocks in breakdown area.
3. Entering "breakdown" area, squeeze your lane.
4. Keep the ball carrier inside and in front of you.

Diagram 2. Lanes on kickoff.

divert and block the tacklers. Often, the coverage team will crisscross running down the field, attempting to confuse a return team that has set its return with specific man-to-man blocking assignments.

For teams kicking off, the coach has to weigh the prospect of (a) booting the ball deep into the end zone and, thus, giving possession to the opposition on the 25-yard line, or (b) risking some of his best special teams players taking big hits and possible injuries while covering a kickoff that comes down short of the end zone. Some coaches, if they have exceptional kick-coverage teams, might purposely not have their kicker put it in the end zone for the automatic touchback, betting their defense can keep the kick-return short of the 25-yard-line. But that's a dangerous attraction; the speed on kickoffs can lead to serious injuries. Most coaches prefer to eliminate the return with the deep kick, spare their covering players the open-field contact and cede the opponent the 25-yard-line start.

"I may be dumb, but I'm not stupid."
— Terry Bradshaw, NFL quarterback

For teams with a limited-range kicker, coaches might elect to kick the just-mentioned "squib" kick, which is harder to handle and, thus, difficult for the return team to set up an effective return. Coaches may decide to use this kind of kick in an effort to keep it out of the hands of an opponent's exceptional return man. The down side of the squib is that it usually affords the return team the prospect of even more yardage in field position — around the 30- to 35-yard-line — than with a longer kick.

If a kickoff goes out of bounds the receiving team has the choice of having the kickoff team kick again after a 5-yard penalty or taking possession on its own 35-yard line.

Gridiron History

An extremely successful high school coach in Arkansas onside kicks after every time his team scores, regardless of the opponent or circumstances. He has figured the odds of recovering the kick are good and the kick puts a great deal of pressure on the receiving team. If his team fails to recover the kick, then it must play great defense to keep the opponent from converting the recovery into points. Since high schools don't have a lot of skilled ball handlers to choose from, an onside kick can more easily work at the high school level where that onside-kicking team, the Pulaski (Arkansas) Academy, won three state titles and posted a 124-22 record in a recent 11-year period.

5.

The Kickoff Return

Kickers are like horse manure. They're all over the place.

— **Johnny McKay, coach, USC**

Although it's one of the most dramatic and game-changing offensive plays in football, the kickoff return is rare today. Why? Because of the increased number of kickers who are able to kick the ball deep in the end zone, causing the returner to decide against attempting a return. The ball is downed, giving his team possession on the 25-yard line. When the rule makers moved the kickoff point back five yards to increase the chances of a return, they also moved the point of possession after a touchback — returner downing the ball in the end zone — five yards farther to the 25-yard line. This was an incentive for kicking teams to kick the ball high and short of the end zone to increase the number of kick returns.

As for the return team, if the ball is to be returned out of the end zone, its coach has to have confidence in the team's blocking and return man to gain at least 25 yards; otherwise the decision to return a kick rather than touching the ball down to start the drive will result in "lost" yardage.

"How do you pick your kickoff returner?"

It's usually an offensive player, but not always; the player needs to be sure handed, fast and able to outmaneuver tacklers in the open field. As a special teams player — those on kicking and receiving teams — the returner also needs to be courageous because those who are covering the kick are coming to tackle him at top speed, often with a sense of vengeance.

"What is a wedge kickoff return?"

When the return team puts two players shoulder-to-shoulder in front of the return man, intending to run over any player who comes across their path. It's a dangerous formation, as the offensive players are large, picked for their brute physical attributes. The most effective wedge starts about 10 yards in front of the returner and runs up the field full speed as the ball is caught. The return man must trust that the wedge will either obliterate or separate any tacklers courageous enough to challenge it. And he must have the courage to get behind his blockers and go full speed, even though it may appear there's no opening. Because of the high-speed collisions with fast, large athletes, the wedge can lead to injuries on both sides of the ball. For those of you wondering where the term "suicide squad" came from, this is where.

Gridiron Tradition: The Wedge Return

In 1892, the famous "Flying Wedge" was developed by Harvard University. The offense divided its unit in half, 20 yards behind the line of scrimmage on either side of the field. On a signal, the two sides started running toward the defense, coming together in a "Flying Wedge" as the quarterback touched the ball down to begin the play and started running behind his blockers. With so much distance between the offense and defense to begin with, and the rules back then allowing the entire offense to be in motion towards the defense before the snap of the ball, there were numerous collisions and numerous injuries. There were even some fatalities. This was also the first time the term "holy shit" was used by the poor souls facing the wedge. By 1894, fearful of the negative image of the violence the press had prompted, mass momentum plays were outlawed.

"What is the 'hands' return team?"

This is a receiving formation of nine to 10 men, each having ball-handling skills and lined up between 10 and 15 yards from the kicker. Coaches use the hands team when they expect a short onside kickoff, usually in the latter stages of a tight game with the kicking team behind on the scoreboard. It's arguably the most exciting single play in football because the shape of the ball guarantees unpredictable and un-expected bounces — with the game often on the line. Unless a player has a "sure thing" recovery, the receiving team doesn't want to touch the ball before it goes 10 yards, after which it is a free ball, with either team eligible to recover. If the front line waits too long to determine if the ball is going the necessary 10 yards, they may be overwhelmed by the covering players on the kickoff. The kicking team's chances of recovering are roughly 60% for surprise onside kicks, but only 20% for expected kicks.

"What are the blocking rules for kickoff returns?"

Blockers may not block a player below the waist or from the back. If the would-be tackler does not see the blocker and is "defenseless by rule," the blocker is prohibited from targeting the upper body of the tackler, which constitutes a "blindside block."

"Can the receiving team call for a fair-catch on a kickoff?"

Yes, in return for an unimpeded chance to catch the kick, the returner gives up his option to run with it. A team trying an onside kick will avoid a high kick that can be fair caught unless aimed at an unguarded area.

"Does the return team try to block every player?"

No, usually a receiving team will have a double-team block at the main point of its return and leave covering players farthest from the return un-blocked, figuring such players can't get to the return point fast enough to make the tackle.

Coaching Points

A return man who bobbles the kickoff in the end zone can fall on it and down it in the end zone without penalty; the ball is put into play on the 25-yard line. If a returner "muffs" a kickoff — never has clear possession — in the field of play and then falls on the ball back in the end zone, it's a touchback, not a safety, and comes out to the 25-yard line.

A good coach makes sure his return man understands the difference as a desperate decision to run a bobbled kickoff out of the end zone can cost a team vital field position or, worse, a turnover or safety. The latter occurs when a player is tackled in his end zone after first possessing the ball outside the end zone, giving the other team two points.

Coaches need to convince players to resist clobbering a would-be tackler who is chasing the ball and not looking at blockers, putting him in a "defenseless position" by rule. To avoid the 15-yard unnecessary roughness penalty for targeting a defenseless player, the blocker should shield or push the tackler away from the ball carrier. It is not the crowd-pleasing, crushing block that players used to dream of, but it's effective and prevents serious injuries such as concussions.

Jerry Thompson

A returner has broken free on a kickoff return, meaning the two teammates behind him must resist the urge to block the pursuing defenders. To do so would likely lead to an unnecessary roughness or a block-in-the-back penalty. Never block behind the ball.

6.

Offense:
By Land

You don't get hurt running straight ahead ... three-yards-and-a-cloud-of-dust offense. I will pound you and pound you until you quit.

— **Woody Hayes, coach, Ohio State**

The offense is the team that has the ball and is running plays to advance it by run or pass towards the opponent's goal line in an attempt to score points in one of two ways: by a touchdown — six points — or by a field goal — three points.

There are 11 players on the offensive team: a quarterback, five offensive linemen and a collection of five receivers and backs who are eligible to catch forward passes.

There must be seven players on the line of scrimmage — the point where the ball is when the play begins — but only the two players on each end of that line are eligible to catch passes.

The five linemen ineligible to catch passes are called interior linemen. Their primary function is to block defensive players, whether it's a running play or a passing play. As a result, these players are the largest on the team, not necessarily fleet of foot, and don't enjoy the limelight like ball handlers do. Then again, you never see them drop passes or fumble the football, since, beyond the center, they almost never touch the ball.

The backs are smaller and much faster than the linemen. They are expected to outmaneuver and run away from defenders attempting to tackle them to the ground, which ends the play at that spot on the field. These players utilize a variety of skills, from throwing and catching to blocking, but usually against players more their own size.

"The only qualifications for a lineman are to be big and dumb. To be a back, you only have to be dumb."

— Knute Rockne, coach, Notre Dame

Coaches use a variety of formations to put these players in positions where they can avoid the defense and score points. To that end, all players on the team have precise responsibilities on every play. A great deal of practice time is spent coordinating the assignments of the different units of players. It takes a lot of time to coordinate the movements of 11 players, many of whom are running in different directions for the same objective.

There are many running offenses in football, as many as the number of coaches who design them. Every coach adds his unique characteristics, based on his preferences and his players' strengths. For our purposes, we will look at three main running systems: power, "run to daylight" and the option.

"What are power running attacks?"

Power running attacks are run out of many different formations, but have three of the same features: a double-team block at the point of attack, a "kick-out" block (see glossary) on the line's end man — either a defensive end or linebacker — and a blocker leading the runner through the hole created by those two blocks. This play can be run best out of the I formation, but coaches have many ways to use different players to execute the kick-out and lead blocking assignments, some running in motion before the snap of the ball to put them in position to make their block.

When you watch a running play be aware that the formation the offense lines up in can be different from the one it's in when the ball is snapped. The double-team block could be a combination of wing back and tight end, tight end and tackle, or tackle and guard, depending on where the coach wants the play to develop. The kick-out block could

Zone Blocking

Players on line step hard right to protect the gaps, then block defenders

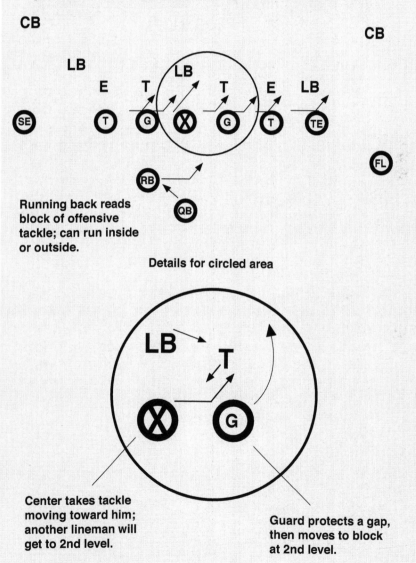

Running back reads block of offensive tackle; can run inside or outside.

Details for circled area

Center takes tackle moving toward him; another lineman will get to 2nd level.

Guard protects a gap, then moves to block at 2nd level.

Diagram 3. Zone blocking.

come from a pulling guard, tight end in motion, or a running back. The lead block could come from a pulling guard, a tight end in motion or a back running in front of the ball carrier.

A team running a power run game ideally has two backs in the backfield and big, strong, mean offensive linemen who get a kick out of "pancaking" defenders who get in their way. The top teams lining up in the I formation in the 1960s ran this system; their defenders knew they were in for some bruising while trying to slow it down.

Today, teams also run power out of a one-running-back formation, the Pistol, where the back lines up behind the quarterback who is three yards directly behind the center. This allows the "tailback" a running start towards the line of scrimmage when he gets the handoff and a better chance to see running lanes that open in front of him.

Good running teams traditionally don't spend a lot of time passing, but because they can force the defense to repeatedly react to bruising run plays, excellent opportunities abound for play-action passes — after faking a run play — that often get receivers wide open because the defenders are hustling to stop another expected off-tackle run. For running teams, the play-action passes won't work unless the run play is consistently successful.

"What does running to daylight mean?"

"Run to daylight" was the term for the legendary Vince Lombardi's Green Bay Packers offense, combining a power blocking element that afforded the running back the option of running in different lanes, depending on where he saw daylight between defenders.

A similar concept is run today with the proliferation of one-back spread offenses that incorporate three or more wide receivers who are positioned 5-15 yards outside their offensive linemen, which forces the defense to line up wide to cover them.

The result is that the defensive players are stretched thin to cover the area where the offense can run. This makes it easier for the offensive linemen to block and lessens the need for a double-team block where they want to run.

The primary one-back spread blocking scheme is zone, where the offensive linemen need to work together at the same time to block any man in an area, not just a particular defender identified before the snap. The running back starts laterally and must be patient looking for the "daylight" to open up between his blockers.

The quarterback option puts stress on the defense: here, a defender is attempting to cover both the pitchman (left) and the quarterback, who faked a pitch and scored.

"How does the option work?"

Unlike a traditional play where the ball carrier is pre-determined, option running plays in one-, two- or three-back formations all have two common characteristics. First, the ball carrier is determined by how the defense lines up or their reactions after the snap of the ball; and, second, there are two or more possible ball carriers who run a pre-determined route designed to put maximum pressure on the defensive alignment.

Option running attacks put a lot of stress on the defense as teams must assign a particular player to cover each option the play presents. Teams that are smaller and less physical use the option to offset those limitations by forcing the defense to be disciplined, which slows it down. The battle can become a game of discipline and it's for those reasons that the service academies — Navy, Army and Air Force — demand discipline every day, every way and on every play. The result? They traditionally enjoy surprising success running their option offenses against more talented, but less disciplined, teams.

Running Backs

Running backs are versatile football players with lots of important responsibilities. They must be strong enough to break tackles at the line of scrimmage and fast enough to outrun pursuing defenders.

They must be good blockers: lead-blocking for another ball carrier or, on a pass play, blocking a "blitzing" — rushing the passer — linebacker who might outweigh them by 50 pounds.

In this day of wide-open offenses, running backs are also expected to be reliable pass catchers, whether those passes are short or long. Besides speed, strength and balance, running backs must read and anticipate running lanes — or creases — opening in what might look to the casual observer to be nothing but a giant pile of defenders.

Running backs are taught to focus on particular lanes or blocks by their offensive linemen to help determine their path on a running play, but it's instincts that separate great runners from good runners.

If you're watching a great running back you'll see that he makes cuts — changes direction — quickly, taking advantage of tacklers who are off balance and making those who aren't miss embarrassingly.

"How do running backs know where to run?"

On a typical running play, the running back looks at the defensive line before the snap for hints of where the hole might be and then, as the ball is snapped, at a "landmark" — say, the outside hip of the tackle in front of him.

If the tackle blocks his man inside, the back knows to cut outside. If the tackle blocks his man to the outside, the back needs to adjust, in a split-second, and run inside.

"What is the mesh point?"

On an option play, it's the point where the quarterback holds the ball against the stomach of a running back while looking at the defense to decide to hand off or keep it himself. It's the responsibility of the quarterback to make that work smoothly when the back has *his* eyes up to read the linemen's blocks.

When the quarterback has *his* eyes up to read the defensive end to give or keep the ball, the running back is then responsible for the mesh. The pressure of the ball in the back's stomach can be very subtle. If a quarterback fakes the handoff and keeps, coaches want the running back to penetrate the line of scrimmage to make the defense think he has the ball; otherwise, he gets a "loafing" grade.

Watch the fakes and see how you would grade the quarterback and running backs; do they fool you?

"What kind of blocking do receivers do?"

Blocking is not as glamorous as dancing in the end zone with a touchdown pass — more like having to pick up the poo of the family dog: necessary, but unpleasant. Most spectators don't watch for it or appreciate the skill involved, but teams that break loose for long runs — "explosion plays" — almost always have receivers who block well down field. When blocking the man over him, a receiver has three choices:

First, if the player reads the back covering him man-to-man and is not looking back at the ball, he can run deep, knowing the defender will run with him. Running off deep defenders also opens the shallow area beyond scrimmage for a short pass to another receiver.

Second, if the cornerback is playing five to 10 yards from him, the receiver can run at him to try and make him back up, and then break down — get under control — at an angle between the defender and the ball, and "stalk block" him. The blocker should have a wide base and try to get his hands into the chest of the defender and drive him backwards. A stalemate is acceptable if the runner is close and the corner can't disengage to make the tackle.

"I believe like I'm the best, but you're not going to get me to say that."
— Jerry Rice, NFL receiver

Third, if the defense is using hard zone coverage — the defender is not going to retreat — the receiver knows he can't drive the corner off the ball. In that case, he takes an inside-out position on the corner and initiates contact, maintaining his balance and driving the defender backwards, giving the ball carrier a running lane. Again, a stalemate is acceptable if it lasts long enough for the ball carrier to get by him.

The rules allow the receiver to use his hands on the "frame" of the defender, which is from the shoulders to waist, limited to the torso. Any use of the hands outside that frame — arms, legs, back — is illegal and, if seen by an official, will result in a penalty of 10 yards for holding. Defenders use their hands to protect themselves and because of how quickly such "hand-fighting" occurs, you'll probably notice a lot of holding goes on without penalty because it's hard for an official to detect it without instant replay. This also happens a good deal along the line of scrimmage in the trenches with the big boys. Referees will sometimes let holding go if it does not have a negative impact on the play.

"What does a receiver need to be an effective blocker?"

A wide receiver needs to not only be competitive — fairly easy — but tough — not so easy. But, at the college level, this is what separates the great receivers from those who were good in high school because they were fast and the competition weak. In college, all defensive backs are tough and they don't like getting blocked by a wide receiver; they feel it's demeaning — like having your pants fall down when your belt breaks. As a result, receivers need "tough love" from their coaches to develop the mental and physical toughness to be a good blocker. As receivers learn to stay square — "face up" — with defensive backs, gain strength in the weight room and get praise for effective blocking, their pride swells. Coaches also know that the tougher the receiver thinks he is, the more aggressive he is at catching the ball.

Gridiron Tradition

The most significant, if obscure, ball carrier of all time was an English schoolboy named William Webb Ellis. In November 1823, he was engaged in a game of football featuring 30 to 40 players on each side attempting to kick a ball over a goal line in Rugby, England. Just like in America at that time, this was the only way to score a goal; players were prohibited from running with the ball in their hands. As the school bell ending the game began to toll, Ellis ran to fair-catch a punt, which would allow him a free kick for goal. His opponents slowed to allow the catch and were then surprised to see Ellis, "with a fine disregard for the rules of football as played in his time first took the ball in his arms and ran with it, originating the distinctive feature of the rugby game."

The opponents were angered at the breach of rules and attempted to bring Ellis to the ground, but he dodged and stiff-armed would-be tacklers and reached the goal on the last stroke of the bell. The young lad was severely criticized for his brazen act but, in time, others saw this as an opportunity for a great innovation to the game, making it more interesting and popular, both to play and watch. Thus was born "the run."

7.

Offense: By Air

There's no thrill like throwing a touchdown pass.

— Joe Montana, NFL quarterback

The forward pass didn't really take flight until the 1930s. At the time, even among gifted quarterbacks, a 50% pass completion rate was rare as teams began to attempt more passes in the Depression and World War II years.

The coaches had not developed the skills of pass protection that could deal with the defenses of the time. With little organized protection, passers were trying to throw while running for their lives.

In the 1940s Paul Brown, coach of the Cleveland Browns, developed a pass-blocking system that insured success and spiked a rise in pass completion rates.

"Cup protection" was the term for Brown's system in which the offensive linemen dropped back, slightly angling their bodies towards the sidelines, forming a cup, and then pushing the incoming pass-rushers outside the cup and away from the quarterback.

The fast-paced, high-scoring games of today are noted for exciting and effective passing attacks that have demolished records in both the professional and college ranks.

As the rules and officials became more lenient in overlooking offensive

Jerry Thompson

Five offensive linemen (in black) drop to form "cup" protection for the passer.

linemen holding in pass protection and stricter in calling defensive pass interference, passing records, and scoring soared in a big way.

Quarterback

The quarterback is the player who receives the ball on the "hike" from the center to start a play. The coaches or backup quarterbacks on the sideline communicate or hand-signal the play to the QB. It's his responsibility to pass this signal on to the rest of the offensive team in the huddle or on the line of scrimmage. Depending on how the defense is lined up, the quarterback may need to make changes to the play, known as an "audible," at the line of scrimmage. This responsibility makes the quarterback position the most important on the offense; he's a decisive influence on whether a team wins or loses.

"All outstanding football teams have two distinct characteristics in common—a great fighting spirit and a great quarterback," said the

Jerry Thompson

Bear Bryant, greatest coach of all time, said: "A smart, capable quarterback is the greatest single asset a football team can possess."

man considered the greatest college coach of all time, Alabama's Bear Bryant. "A smart, capable quarterback is the greatest single asset a football team can possess."

Bryant said there were three types of quarterbacks, the best being, "The one every coach is seeking. He directs his team to maximum results. He is a student of the game. He is logical in his thinking and bold in his action, when necessary … . He is confident, and gives his team confidence in him and the offense. He is a winner through preparation, and he will give you winners through action and leadership."

"What are the physical qualities of a great quarterback?"

Such a quarterback will have all the qualities attributed by Bryant, plus a few more. Usually the quarterback is fairly tall, which is important given the tall defenders who raise their hands as they rush him while he's looking for uncovered receivers in the secondary. Height is particularly important in throwing balls "over the middle" as opposed to passes to his left or right flanks.

"Sure, luck means a lot in football. Not having a good quarterback is bad luck."
— Don Shula, coach Miami Dolphins

A good quarterback needs to have a quick release and those who do keep the ball chest high, with two hands protecting it before they throw. If you see a quarterback drop the ball down waist high, winding up to throw the ball, you'll likely see some interceptions. The motion gives away his throwing intentions to the defense and is slow — it shows the quarterback needs to generate momentum to make up for his lack of arm strength.

Vision is an absolute must for a quarterback. He needs to be able to judge the speed — distance — of all those receivers and defenders, while looking past the gorillas that are trying to tackle him before he can throw. As young quarterbacks throw interceptions to opponents instead of completions to teammates they thought were open, their vision — and experience — expands peripherally. This is the major challenge for high school quarterbacks going on to college and college quarterbacks moving to the pros. At each level defensive players are faster and better athletes, which means they can cover more distance when the ball is thrown. Coaches of rookie quarterbacks need to be cautious in how they push them — sometimes players have to live with their mistakes to get better.

Along with vision, depth perception is a major element of accuracy. The quarterback must be able to judge his receiver's speed and "lead"— throw the ball so he doesn't have to slow down to catch it.

"Three things can happen when you throw the ball, and two of them are bad."

— Darrell Royal, Texas coach — and lots of other coaches

The quarterback also needs to be strong and durable because he will take some punishing hits, even when he completes a pass. Having some speed as a runner is important, as is the ability to scramble — to elude pass rushers. Finally, he must be smart — exceptionally smart. Quarterbacks need to all but live in the film room, observing and absorbing the opponent's strengths and weaknesses — and be able to put all that into practice on the field. "Game manager" is a term you'll hear regarding an effective quarterback who, during the chaos of a fast-moving game, makes good decisions and few mistakes.

"When the quarterback comes to the line of scrimmage, what is going through his mind?"

First, the quarterback scans the defense to make sure the play called is appropriate for the defense he sees in front of him. If he's not convinced, he must change the play — remember, that's an "audible" — to one that has a better chance of success. The quarterback has only seconds to do this evaluation. The defensive players may be moving around and yelling instructions to each other — perhaps even throwing some verbal taunts the QB's way. Meanwhile, the crowd may be roaring. Despite all this, the quarterback must be able to focus and cull, from all the information he studied prior to the game, whether to stick with the play or change it.

Second, once he makes that call, the quarterback must remember his individual keys for that particular play. When the ball is snapped, he needs to have his vision on the correct defensive players to make the proper decision about, say, whether to hand off the ball or keep it himself — and, in

QB's Pass Progression
Quarterback decides if priority route is open.
If not, he must move to the next option.

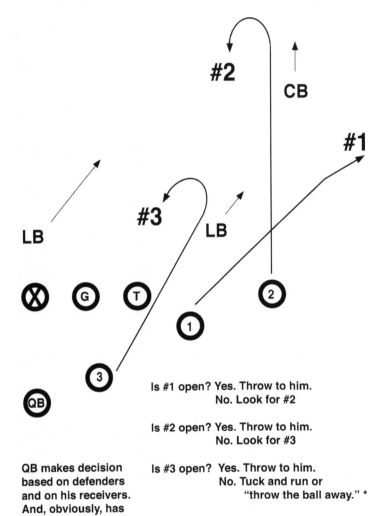

Is #1 open? Yes. Throw to him.
No. Look for #2

Is #2 open? Yes. Throw to him.
No. Look for #3

QB makes decision
based on defenders
and on his receivers.
And, obviously, has
to decide in a hurry.

Is #3 open? Yes. Throw to him.
No. Tuck and run or
"throw the ball away." *

* Throw an intentional incompletion to avoid being
sacked and, thus, taking a loss of yardage.

Diagram 4. Pass progression for quarterbacks.

passing situations, about which receiver he should throw to.

Games are often won or lost on decisions made by the quarterback. There are two kinds of audibles: "must checks" and "advantage checks." Does the QB recognize a blitz — the defense sending extra (five or more) players to rush a suspected pass attempt — and change the play accordingly (*"must"* check)? Does he exploit a substitute at defensive back who might have difficulty covering a particular pass receiver (*"advantage"* check)? Does he recognize when a receiver is well covered and resist throwing to him, even if that might have been the play he called? All of these split-second decisions — and the reality that he must make them on every single play — underscores why this position is the most important on the field.

"How do defenses try to harass the quarterback?"

Defenses may choose to give the quarterback — and the coaches in the press box — a blitz look and then back out of it on the snap of the ball. This disguise can be effective as evidenced by a school's recent success against an outstanding quarterback, who in two years, completed 44 passes against the team (a lot) but for only 6.9 yards per completion (not a lot). Eleven yards would be average and 6.9 is not good enough to beat anybody. To confuse and unsettle a quarterback, a team might have its defensive backs and linebackers move around prior to the snap. The longer the quarterback takes to figure out what's happening, the better it is for the defensive players rushing the passer and the secondary covering the receivers.

Gridiron History

In early football, with the compacted formations of the single wing and other power running formations, the quarterback was not lined up in the usual position of today; he lined up behind the guard and barked out the signals. The center would snap the ball to the tailback, who was 5-7 yards behind the line of scrimmage, where the quarterback is now in the shotgun formation. At that time, the quarterback rarely handled the ball and was mostly used as a blocker, much like a fullback in today's offenses.

Wide Receiver

Teams will use up to five wide receivers at a time with a wide-open passing offense — two ends on the line and three players in the backfield. These wide receivers are a variety of heights and weights, but all should have speed, quickness and sure hands. Receivers are known mainly for the ability to get open against either "man-to-man" — defensive players cover a

Wide Receivers' Passing Tree

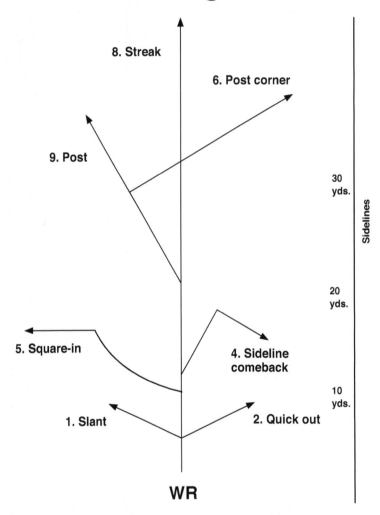

For this team, even-numbered routes go
toward the sideline, odd-numbered go away.
The higher the number, the deeper the route.

Diagram 5. The Passing Tree.

specific receiver — or "zone" — defensive players cover an area of the field — pass defense, but a recent trend is also the player's ability as a blocker.

Most teams have a split end who lines up on the line of scrimmage outside an offensive tackle. If the tight end is replaced by another wide receiver, he will be required to line up on the line of scrimmage also. Remember that in every offensive formation there must be at least seven players on the line of scrimmage, with only the two outside eligible to catch passes. A big mistake can be when three eligible receivers are lined up on the line of scrimmage along with the five linemen. If the play is a run, it's okay: you can have more than seven players on the line of scrimmage. But if it's a pass, the middle receiver has been made ineligible by the wide receiver to his side also lining up on the line of scrimmage — only the outside receivers on the line of scrimmage are eligible receivers.

Great gains have been called back when a split end is sent in as a flanker — the widest receiver *off* the line of scrimmage — and forgets to line up off the ball, especially in a late-game desperation drive. Well-coached teams have their split ends and flankers check with the side officials who will let them know if they are on the line of scrimmage.

Counting the quarterback, who can become a receiver after he hands off or laterals to someone else, it's possible to have three more wide receivers in various formations aligned at least a yard behind the ball, off the line of scrimmage. Most teams will not use this many receivers unless they feel they can surprise the defense, which might leave one or more uncovered. The most productive offenses still leave at least one running back in every formation to block for the quarterback and to serve as a running threat against defenses that might otherwise position their players for only a pass.

"How many pass patterns does a receiver know how to do?"

Perhaps seven or more. Most receivers have short, medium and deep routes. Short routes are from three to seven yards: a "hitch", where the receiver, drives the cornerback and suddenly turns to the quarterback who throws it very quickly; a "quick out," where the receiver turns toward the sideline where the quarterback leads him away from the defensive back; and a "quick post," where the receiver sprints off the ball, head-fakes to the outside and cuts inside looking for a quick pass from the quarterback. These three routes require only a three-step drop by the quarterback taking a direct snap from center before he throws.

Coaches like these kinds of routes against soft zone coverage — corner defenders lined up deeper than 8 yards; tight "man" coverage; and blitz situations where the ball is thrown quickly before the pass rushers can get to the quarterback. Offensive line coaches also like this kind of pass because it's quick and takes pressure off the linemen's need to protect the quarterback for longer periods of time.

Medium routes are similar, just longer — in the 10- to 17-yard yard range. Many of these routes are called against zone pass coverage, so the receivers need more time to find, and get to, an open area. A quarterback might drop back five to seven steps from the line of scrimmage to help better time his throws with receivers going deeper. The linemen know they must hold their blocks longer.

Long routes are called "streaks" and "posts." On the former, the receiver runs at the defender, fakes another route in hopes of "freezing" him, then bursts down field for the deep throw. On the latter, the receiver releases like a streak but then cuts inside, toward the goal posts.

A common error with the streak route is that the receiver straightens up and doesn't get close enough to the defender before making his deep break, allowing the corner to "read" — anticipate — his route and, thus, turn and match the receiver stride for stride. Another common error? Running too closely to the sideline — three to five yards is good — and not allowing the quarterback room to hit him in bounds.

The deep post is a must for the dangerous receiver as he drives the corner off, makes a head-and-shoulder fake and cuts inside and behind any player trying to defend the middle.

As with the streak, the receiver must use his speed to get close enough to the defender so that when he makes his final cut, the back doesn't have time to pivot and keep up with him.

"When is a receiver ineligible to catch a pass?"

When he goes out of bounds — unless he was forced out by a defensive player and immediately attempts to get back inbounds. Passes completed in this fashion usually must go through an instant-replay review before being determined to be complete because the referee may have only seen the receiver come back inbounds and missed the part where he was pushed out by the defensive back. Once the pass is touched by a defensive player or official, everyone is eligible to catch it, even the big linemen.

8.

Offense:
By Foot

I recruited a Czech kicker, and during the eye exam, when asked to read the bottom line, the kicker replied, "Read it? I know him."

— **Woody Hayes, coach, Ohio State**

Kickers are, without question, the loneliest players on the team. No one wants to sit next to them on the bench, partly because they aren't considered "regular" players, partly because they tend to be loners and partly because they don't want to be jinxed. Beyond the quarterback, kickers are the most likely players to influence the outcome of the game — in their cases, by kicks in critical situations. Make it and they're the hero; miss it and they're the goat.

"What does a place kicker do?"

The place kicker kicks extra points after touchdowns, field goals and kickoffs. Such players come in all shapes and sizes; in most cases, it does help to have some size and weight to get behind the ball.

Through the 1970s most kickers kicked straight-on with their toe, but that's given way to the soccer-style kick, from the side, produced with the instep of the kicker. This change coincided with the growth and popularity of soccer and the coming realization that physics favor the wider impact

Jerry Thompson

The offensive linemen interlock their feet to eliminate gaps defenders who might rush through to block a field goal.

area of the foot for accuracy. The toe was a small impact point and the straight-ahead approach was limited in the short arc of the kicker's leg coming into the ball. Soccer style, on the other hand, offers a larger mass on the ball and the sidewinding approach offers a bigger arc and more speed, which equals higher, longer kicks with the same amount of approach steps.

"Who is the player holding the ball for the kicker?"

It's usually the "best friend" of the kicker, who depends on the guy to catch the snap from the center and place the tip of the ball — laces toward the goal posts — upright on the ground in good position to kick, all in a split-second. The holder must have quick and reliable hands because the ball comes to him fast, and with "mustard on it." From snap to kick, 1.2 seconds would be a good time.

Charlie Brown of "Peanuts" cartoon fame is fooled every year by his holder, Lucy, who promises to hold the ball for him to kick. Every year, she takes the ball away at the last second, leaving him frustrated. A kicker can injure his knee if the holder drops the ball right before he kicks it. For that reason, the holder is usually a quarterback because he is used to handling center snaps, although many teams use their punter for the same reason.

Punters also have more time to work with the kicker while the rest of the team is practicing offense and defense.

"What are the fundamentals for a good place kicker?"

The skills of a kicker are very much like those of a great golfer. He needs to be able to keep his head down and follow through with his kick while blocking out the noise of the crowd and the pursuit of the defensive team attempting to block his kick or rattle him with nasty remarks about his mother. Kickers must be strong mentally, especially when their attempt can decide the outcome of a game.

Kickers are known to be superstititous, but the overall rule is don't go near them when they're preparing for a crucial field goal; it's like not mentioning "no-hitter" to a pitcher who is working on one.

Most kickers will use the same two-to-three steps for field goals and extra points and five-to-10-yard approach for kickoffs. In decisive situations, opposing coaches will often call a timeout right before the snap for a field goal, hoping to "ice" the kicker into choking and missing the kick after the timeout. This tactic became customary as coaches' jobs began to depend more on whether the other team's kickers made their kicks or not.

"What constitutes a good kickoff?"

Most coaches prefer a kickoff that goes into and out of the return team's end zone, giving the offense the ball at the 25 yard-line. In such cases, there is no return possibility and the covering team doesn't have to get involved in as many heavy-hitting blocks while running down the field.

If a coach does not have a kickoff man with enough length to kick to the end zone, he will have the kicker aim for inside the sideline to one side of the field or another. In this way, his players don't have to cover the far side of the field and can compress their numbers to cover the other two-thirds — though the risk is the kicker kicking the ball out of bounds, which gives the offense great field position at the 35-yard-line. A kickoff that comes down in the middle of the field is dangerous because the return team can choose to return it left or right or up the middle. This threat puts more pressure on the covering players to stay in their respective lanes and thus spreads the coverage thin compared to a kickoff into the corner of the field.

"Can kickers tackle the ball carrier?"

Most kickers are eager to stay out of the way of the ball carrier because they're not physical like defenders. Coaches will have the kicker be a safety

Jerry Thompson

The punter kicks with his instep like a place kicker, but with an up-and-down kicking motion rather than sideways. Both must concentrate on kicking while there are defenders in their face attempting to block their kicks.

covering behind the first wave, attempting to make the runner cut back towards other tacklers if he breaks through. Watch the kicker cover kickoffs from time-to-time; it can be interesting and entertaining all at once. That's because when it comes to tackling, a kicker is like a homeowner checking on a possible burglar downstairs: hoping against hope that nobody is there because, deep down, he doesn't really want to get involved.

"How do punters kick the ball?"

The punter uses his instep like the soccer style kicker, but as his leg swings towards the ball, aims his foot more "up," attempting to produce more "hang time" — time the kicked ball is in the air — so that his teammates covering the kick have time to get to the return man before he catches it. An ideal punt, from snap to kick would be 2.5 seconds and would be in the air for at least 4.5 seconds, giving ample time for at least some of his teammates to elude blocks and run some 40 yards to stop the returner.

In recent years, coaches have recruited rugby-style punters, who catch the ball and run with it laterally behind a wave of two or three blockers, buying time for the other coverage players to run downfield before he punts the ball. This tactic has dramatically reduced the number of punt returns because the coverage gets to the returner before the ball does. This is an interesting development as it takes the play back to the original roots of American football: the rugby game, which is still played worldwide.

"What is a long snapper?"

The player who snaps the ball back to the holder for a place kick and the punter for a punt is the long snapper. Usually a lineman, the long snapper is a specialist who has the same characteristics a good pitcher has in baseball — strong wrists and the ability to put spin on a ball that he throws backwards through his legs.

"You need two yards, I'll get you three. You need 10 yards, I'll get you three."

— Leroy Hoard, NFL football player

Snappers will warm up and practice by cocking both wrists and flinging the ball overhead to another player up to 15-20 yards away. Good long snappers must be accurate, able to snap the ball to their target — the punter or holder's hands — quickly and consistently, no matter the weather or game conditions. An acceptable snap for a punt would be between .65 to .8 seconds and .5 to .6 seconds for a place kick. College teams may award a scholarship to a long snapper who does not play any other position. Because of his limited responsibility, he is able to practice by himself and with the kickers while the rest of the team is practicing offense and defense.

In early times, the defense would take advantage of the long snapper having his head down, looking back at the kicker while he was snapping the ball by colliding and knocking the center backwards. This made life dangerous for snappers and, because of head injuries, the rules changed so the rushing team can't run over the top of the center while he's snapping the ball. This was necessary protection and allowed the snapper to concentrate on his job.

George Allen, once head coach of the Washington Redskins, was known as a special teams "guru" in the 1960s. He picked his center snapper by his ability to spin the ball the same rate on a place kick so it would hit the holder's hands with the laces facing the goal posts every time. With the laces facing forward, it was easier for the kicker to kick a ball straight, without any sideways wobble. Both punters and place kickers are renowned for idiosyncratic personalities and superstitions. Long snappers fit in with that group nicely.

"What are the average sizes of college offensive football players?"

Quarterbacks: 6-2, 210 pounds.
Running backs: 5-11, 205 pounds.
Fullbacks: 6-0, 234 pounds.
Wide receivers: 6-1, 193 pounds.
Tight ends: 6-4, 244 pounds.
Offensive linemen: 6-4, 298 pounds.

High school players' sizes vary greatly as a result of youngsters not having fully developed physically. Lower levels of college competition have more players who aren't as tall or fast as Division 1A players.

Size and speed are the two most important standards by which nearly all major college players are evaluated and recruited. Pro players are bigger and, in the first years of their careers, faster than most college players. Once professionals pass their 26th birthday, they tend to slow down as age, injuries and life's distractions take their inevitable toll.

9.

Blocks
of Granite

Football linemen are motivated by a more complicated, self-determining series of factors than the single fear of humiliation in the public gaze which is the emotion that galvanizes the backs and receivers.

— **Merlin Olsen, NFL All-Pro lineman**

In 1936, the offensive line at Fordham University in New York was given a nickname that says it all when it comes to offensive linemen: "the (forgotten) Seven Blocks of Granite." Little glory, but lots of blood, sweat and tears. And, often, the difference between a team winning and losing.

The Center

This is the player on the line of scrimmage who "hikes" — snaps — the ball to the quarterback to start each play. Two linemen called guards flank the center on either side. The center may snap the ball by a "direct" snap, with the quarterback's hands between his legs, or a "shotgun" snap to the quarterback about five yards behind him. There was some delicacy involved with the evolution of the direct snap: quarterbacks were unsure about where they were putting their hands — and hoping the center hadn't stopped at Smiley's House of Sauerkraut for the "all-you-can-eat-buffet" before practice.

The center must be a versatile athlete with a good understanding of the overall blocking schemes for run and pass plays. Before the snap, you'll often see the center pointing to a defensive player to show his teammates the blocking pattern for that particular play. Sometimes, when the defensive line moves before the snap of the ball, the center must alert his mates to change the blocking to meet that change.

> ### *"Being in politics is like being a football coach. You have to be smart enough to understand the game and dumb enough to think it's important."*
>
> — **Eugene McCarthy, politician**

It will help you to get a pencil and paper to diagram the following, — the offensive players are o's and the defensive players are x's — : a center flanked by each guard, with a defensive lineman over each guard:

If the center is uncovered — no one lined up directly over him — watch his three main blocking angles on running plays.

One, he will fire up field to cut off a linebacker.

Two, he will block "back" on the man over the left guard, away from the direction of the play. This allows the guard, who usually is faster, to be able to pull — to the right — off the line of scrimmage and block a defender outside the formation.

Three, the center will fire off laterally and double-team the defender over the right guard in the same direction of the play. In this situation, the center aims to get over far enough, and quick enough, to block the man over the guard by himself, which frees the guard to leave that defender to the center and move up field to pick off a linebacker

When you watch a top-rate offensive line, keep your eye on the center. There are times when he is uncovered and the play will call for him to pull and block some defender outside, which is unusual in that many centers don't have the speed and athletic ability to do that. When you see a center pull and lead the blocking on an outside play, you're watching a very talented football player.

For that reason, offensive line coaches often believe in getting their best athlete at the center position. Obviously, that ability also helps the potential of successful "onside" — to the direction of the play — double teams with the guards.

"When there's a fumbled snap, who's to blame?"

When the center's nose is covered — by a defender directly over him — it's a problem because he must single-block the nose man and still snap the ball to the quarterback, either by a shot gun snap or direct snap.

In such situations, it's not unusual to see the center's snap become erratic, often delivered too high or low. This is every center's nightmare: short yardage or goal-line situations with the quarterback taking a direct snap and a defender crowding the center's nose or threatening him in the gap between him and the guard.

In this case, the center must remember his first responsibility is to get the ball to the quarterback's hands, not block the defender threatening him. Often a quarterback is blamed for a fumble on the snap when it was the center's fault because he focused on his block first and left the ball short of the quarterback's hands.

When you're watching a game, check out both team's center play; it's the pivotal point in the battle of the trenches.

"With loud crowd noise and the offense in the shotgun formation, how do centers know when to snap the ball?"

Called the "silent snap," it started with NFL quarterback Peyton Manning of the Indianapolis Colts. Let's say the prearranged snap count was on three. Amid the noise, Manning's center would look back through his legs at the quarterback while the rest of the offensive line watched the center's head. The center lifting his head triggered a silent snap count and, on three, the ball would be snapped. The technique demands rhythm and cadence, but once learned, is simple.

Watch the center as he eyes the quarterback; when he lifts his head up, looking at the defense, count to yourself, "one thousand one," etc., until the snap. See if that count is always the same.

Sometimes, this method can be a problem if defensive players catch on to the system, do their own counting and know precisely when the ball will be snapped. If the offense is smart, it will vary the count occasionally to prevent defenders from "teeing off" on the center and breaching gaps on the line of scrimmage.

Offensive Guard

Two guards line up directly on either side of the center. Like the rest of the interior linemen, their job is to block on both running and passing plays. On some plays, rather than blocking straight ahead, a guard will "pull," dropping back out of his position in the line to be the lead blocker for a ball carrier, for traps (inside runs), sweeps (outside runs) or screens (short pass plays behind the line of scrimmage).

In such cases, he's referred to as a "pulling guard." Many times guards are working to double team defenders with either the center or the offensive tackle to their side. Guards are typically shorter than tackles and, because of their need to pull on running plays, frequently the fastest of the interior linemen. (OK, let's be honest: *less slow* than the other interior lineman; it's like comparing an elephant to a rhino.)

"What's the difference between run and pass blocking?"

Run blocking is done by aggressively moving forward with the idea of pushing the defenders backwards and to the ground. Blockers need to have lower shoulder pad levels than the defenders they are blocking to take advantage of leverage and power.

Pass blocking is the same with pad level, but is more passive, as the blocker retreats, forming a half circle, or cup, with the other linemen to protect the quarterback. The defenders, in essence, come to them rather than vice versa. Run and pass blocking can be man-to-man — blocking a designated defender — or zone — blocking anyone in a designated area. There is aggressiveness required in both kinds of blocking, but good pass blocking is harder to do because it requires more patience and finesse.

Offensive Tackle

A tackle plays outside each guard on the line of scrimmage. A team could have an unbalanced line — more linemen on one side of the center. Often you'll see two tackles side by side, blocking on running and pass plays. Coaches do this to press a physical advantage when they have bigger, stronger linemen.

The area from one tackle to the other is an area called the "blocking zone" in which otherwise illegal blocks from behind — blocking an opponent from behind — are allowed. For a right-handed quarterback, the left tackle is charged with protecting him from being hit from behind — known as the QB's "blind side" — and this is usually the most skilled player of the interior line. The tackle may occasionally "pull" on a running play when he is on the same side of the formation as the tight end. Tackles are usually the tallest of the interior offensive linemen because of the emergence of tall defensive ends who are pass-rush threats. They must have good footwork and balance skills because they often block one of the best athletes on the defensive team.

"Why don't offensive linemen get more recognition?"

First, because no statistics, beyond penalties, are kept on them, making it hard to compare and contrast who's good and who's not.

And, second, because spectators focus on the ball. While you're watching your favorite team play, understand that offensive linemen tend to be more cerebral than their counterparts on defense. That's because they have to do more recognition of formations before the ball is snapped and often must switch blocking responsibilities after the ball has been snapped.

"Hey, the offensive linemen are the biggest guys on the field, they're bigger than everybody else, and that's what makes them the biggest guys on the field."
— John Madden, coach Oakland Raiders

Defensive linemen line up the same nearly every play relative to the offensive formation, despite the variety of looks the backs and receivers may present. An offensive lineman may have one assignment for the defense, but needs to switch assignments with a teammate based on the reactions of the defensive line as the ball is snapped. And they need to do this as a five-man unit!

To be an offensive lineman and run the fast-paced offense of today requires these players to be big, strong, fast, smart and durable. Teams run a lot of no-huddle plays with little rest between plays, and that's hard for big guys. Offensive line coaches must develop some depth at the five-line positions and often substitute on the run, much like hockey coaches do. Watch the big offensive tackles, who are also key blockers on screen passes and must be agile enough to push around smaller, quicker players — defensive backs and linebackers — as they try to stop the play.

Traditionally, the most important offensive tackle is the one on the left side of a right-handed passer. That's because the quarterback will usually have his back turned to the left, and can't see the threat of his tackle missing a block on a defensive end who's slathering at the mouth to sack him. This position began getting a lot of attention in the pro game in the 1980s as great NFL rushers such as Lawrence Taylor gained a lot of attention — cash and stats — while sacking the quarterback from the blind side.

Tight End

A versatile athlete, the tight end needs to have the size and blocking ability of an offensive lineman and the agility and finesse of a wide receiver. The tight end is a key blocker on all running plays and must commit to the mentality of the offensive line: a cog in a team within a team, struggling in a physical battle that is anything but glamorous. But, at times, he must break free of the line of scrimmage, avoid linebackers and beat defensive backs one-on-one in a pass-running route to catch a ball thrown by the quarterback.

Athletic tight ends with quickness can be a big asset to the coach who wants to run a simple play out of a variety of formations. Initially called an "H-back," the tight end was a combination of fullback, tight end and pulling guard. The H-back could line up, shift or go in motion, giving the defense fits because it wants to "declare" the offensive formation's strength so it can modify its lineup to best defend that area of strength. But that's difficult when the player you normally use to declare the strength won't sit still long enough to make the calls.

Today, since the H-back is usually a tight end, that's how he's listed. His assignments are to execute the kick-out block on defensive ends (big guys) and outside linebackers (slightly smaller) in the power run game and lead-block for the ball carrier on inside linebackers (big guys) on inside runs. If he's lucky he might be in the newspaper photo when the ball carrier scores, but he probably won't be identified in the picture's cut line. If his coach is creative and uses his tight end for more than blocking, he can place the mobile tight end in a variety of positions all over the field to generate plenty of "face time" opportunities with the media.

Because of the two-way nature of the position, tight ends split their practice time in the running game with the offensive line (usually hard work and no fun) and the quarterbacks and wide receivers in the passing game (always fun).

10.

Communication and Signals

Football combines the two worst things about America: it is violence punctuated by committee meetings.

— **George Will, columnist**

Ten years ago, football was played at a fairly consistent, predictable pace, with both the offense and defense forming a huddle after a play and calling their next play.

Plays might be signaled in by coaches or players on the sidelines or brought in by a player or players substituting for someone already in the game.

Today, offensive plays are sent in by radio to the quarterback in the pros, and by a variety of means in the college game. Coaches or players on the sidelines signal plays to those on the field. One signaler might call the formation and another the play, while others signal in dummy calls to confuse opponents trying to decipher the play.

Hand signals and pictures — everything from *Brady Bunch* photos to mug shots of ESPN hosts — are also used, something former Oregon Coach Chip Kelly began and caught on across the country. The signal callers will wear a bright-colored hat, jersey or sweater that stands out among the players and coaches on the sideline so they can easily be identified by players on the field.

"Who does the signaling of plays from the sideline?"

You can waste a lot of time watching the signalers on the sideline, but occasionally, do it, because it can be entertaining. If you see the quarterback looking away from the sidelines back to his offense you can bet that all those signals that are still being signaled are fakes. If you see the whole offense looking to the sidelines, it could mean that each position group is getting its own signal from a separate coach or player. As in baseball, where opponents try to guess the signals of the other team, the signaling team can try to dissuade such signal-stealing antics by having an "indicator" that signals "the next signal you get is the one I want and all the rest are fake." This puts a premium on discipline in recognition and execution for the team depending on signals from the sidelines.

"How do teams use, or not use, the huddle?"

In the past, opponents might use the huddle to try and trick and confuse: the offense might have had more than 11 players in the huddle and taken the extra ones off the field as they broke the huddle. This would handicap a coach trying to call defenses based on the personnel the offense was fielding. This was made illegal and is now cause for a 5-yard illegal substitution penalty on the offense. At other times, coming together in a huddle can help calm down and refocus an offense that is struggling. Now, with fast-paced offenses, as soon as one play is over and the offense lines up quickly without a huddle and without substituting, the referees will mark the ball in play whether the defense is ready or not.

"What does it sound like in the huddle?"

The quarterback, getting the play from the coach, might say *"OK, boys, third and five* (down and distance needed). *We need this. Doubles right jet* (formation, motion by receiver) *48* (play called: quick pitch to the running back around the right end) *on two* (snap count)." The center might repeat, *"On two, ready, break"* (all clap hands together and break for the line of scrimmage).

When the game is going badly, there might be arguing and blaming going on between players. That's when player leadership and maturity are so important — to refocus the team. Successful teams have players on both offense and defense who are able to shore up younger or weaker players to maintain the discipline needed to play hard and win, especially when the game may not be going their way. Usually it's a quarterback who's granted license to criticize or challenge his teammates when necessary; the rest of the players understand that this comes with the quarterback's position as leader of the offense.

Gridiron History

The first offensive team huddle in college football was implemented, ironically, by the Gallaudet School for the Deaf, in Washington, D.C., in the 1890s. Worried that the opponent could see their signals, the Gallaudet team formed a circled huddle so they could maintain their secrecy. The Gallaudet team also used a drum pounded on their sidelines for a snap count, with all players focusing on the vibrations they could sense from the drum sound. Teams initiated a variety of huddles from that point on: circles, semi-circles, box and choir formations. In some cases, breaking the huddle became a choreographed signature, with the serpentine huddle of UCLA and the "all-turnaround" of Washington being prime examples in the early 1960s.

In the 1950s Paul Brown, coach of the National Football League Cleveland Browns, would call plays from the sideline and have an offensive linemen run it to the quarterback in the huddle. This was unusual as, back then, quarterbacks, not coaches, called plays. The calls by the quarterback were a result of at least a week of preparation with coaches: watching game film, learning tendencies and understanding the game plan, which was mostly developed by the coaching staff during the week's preparation.

Today, while coaches call plays, some game plans are initiated a year in advance of a special football game.

Fast-Paced Offenses

Today, many offensive teams line up on the line of scrimmage without a huddle, looking to the sideline for signals from coaches or designated signal callers. As a result, the defense can't afford to huddle as they might be caught by an offense's quick start. The defense has a hard time keeping up with a fast-pace offense because they have to regroup after the previous play, line up correctly and recognize a new formation, all in a matter of 10 to 15 seconds. Defending a drive of more than five to six plays against a fast-pace offense can exhaust a defense; when Oregon pioneered such offenses, some defenses were so desperate for a break that players would fake injuries so a timeout would be called and they'd get a breather. The defensive coach must have the depth to be able to substitute on the fly.

On the other hand, if the offense substitutes a player, you will see a referee step in and prevent the center from snapping the ball until the defense has an opportunity to match the substitution. This was a rule change made after the no-huddle offenses gained popularity. Defenses were unable to keep up and often had too many, or too few, players on the field for the next play, which provided an unfair advantage to the offense.

Now, if there's no substitution the defense has to suck it up and get lined up quickly. At times, too quickly; you'll see tired, disorganized defenses that become easy pickings for the organized and well-conditioned offense. A defensive coach must anticipate and substitute immediately after the play and, perhaps, use an occasional timeout to rest his team at critical times.

Coaching Points

Most coaches want only the quarterback to talk in the huddle; otherwise, time is wasted. The offense has only 40 seconds to get its next play snapped. Sometimes, other players will give the quarterback information he might need in making the next play call, but it must be done quickly, and, ideally, before the whole offense is huddled. A respected quarterback might also use humor or sarcasm to help bring his team together; this is an intangible that separates great leaders from the ordinary. The quarterback who sees the coach signal in a quarterback sweep against a tough, gigantic defense and says to the huddled offense, "You could get seriously killed out here," before he calls the play, gets a laugh and helps focus his team for the next play. Or before calling a pass play, he might look one of his linemen in the eye and say, "If your man hits me again, I'm going to kick your ass!"

Audible

An audible, as mentioned earlier, is a series of words shouted at the line of scrimmage by the quarterback who changes the play called by the coach to another play that might have a better chance of success. Coaches spend a lot of time with film, charting opponent tendencies on film. They note certain situations: down-and-distance, formation or field position and where defenses show an inclination for certain coverages or defensive fronts. All these help a quarterback decide when to get spontaneous in changing things up at the last minute.

Many teams' offenses have a standard audible that doesn't require the quarterback to change the play at the line of scrimmage; it depends on sight recognition of the defense as they line up for a play. This is effective because fans make a lot of noise when their team is on defense, which can hamper the ability of offensive players to hear the quarterback change the play.

"Are all audibles spoken out loud?"

No. Watch an offense any time they align three wide receivers to the side of the formation and the defense aligns only two defensive backs to cover them (usually zone coverage); the receivers will recognize that only two defensive backs are covering and run a quick screen-pass route. In that case, the quarterback disregards the run play by firing the ball to the wide receiver without saying a word to the rest of the team. It depends totally on visual recognition by the receivers and the quarterback. If the quarterback doesn't see them, and doesn't throw, the receivers still do the screen. That attracts defensive backs to cover them, preventing the defenders from being prepared to stop the run.

Some defensive teams know of this adjustment and show the quarterback two defenders in coverage when they line up. On the snap, they run a third defender from the inside or deep, giving them enough people to stop the play. It doesn't help that if the wide receivers are late recognizing this adjustment, they may be physically overwhelmed at the point of attack. In this way, the defense baits the offense into running a play into the teeth of its defense.

You might wonder why a team wouldn't always line up three defenders to the offensive trips (three receivers) formation. The answer is that coaches believe they must try and "cheat" a defender from pass coverage to help stop the run. Why? Because if they have three defenders out on the receivers, they are one man short to cover all the gaps in the run defense.

11.

Punting

When in doubt, punt.

— John Heisman, coach

When the offensive team fails to make a first down in three plays, it has a decision to make: go for the yardage needed on fourth down or punt — kick — the ball as far as possible towards the opponent's goal line and try to prevent a run back.

The punter lines up about 15 yards behind the line of scrimmage, closer if he's squeezed by having to kick from his own end zone. After receiving the hike from center, or "long snapper," he kicks the football high and far in an attempt to pin the opponent as deeply in its own territory as possible.

The punter must be skilled in angling the football and/or kicking it as high as possible — called "hang time" — to limit a punt returner's chance of a run back. The punter kicks the ball with his instep, literally off the side of his foot. If he places it just right on the kicking foot, he can make the ball spiral and make the nose turn over in flight, giving the punt more distance. As mentioned, players are increasingly using a "rugby-style" kick, in which the punter runs outside the offensive tackle and then kicks the ball. He may actually use his toe to get some "English" on the ball's flight and on the bounce once it hits the ground. Punting this way markedly restricts opponents' punt block and punt return attempts because the punter kicks from different spots each time and therefore is unpredictable. This method also gives the covering players more time to get down field to tackle the punt returner.

What's more, the punter might try to make the ball spin or tumble in an unusual way, making it harder to catch and possibly leading to a muff or fumble that the punter's team can recover.

"What is hang time?"

Hang time is how long the kicked ball remians in the air. Ideal hang time is figured by dividing the length of the kick by tenths of a second. A 45-yard punt should ideally take 4.5 seconds. The linear relationship (of yardage by tenths of a second) drops off after a 50-yard punt but hang-times of 5 seconds and a little more are still considered great punts.

Today, more teams are giving up the strategy of hang time for shorter punts by kickers who may run sideways (like a rugby kick) before kicking short with forward action on the ball to give the covering players more time to race forward to down the ball closer to the goal line.

The punt may actually be too short to be caught by the punt returner and may cover more yardage rolling on the ground than it does in the air. This strategy is also used to negate the speed and running skills of a great punt returner as the landing and catching, point of the kick becomes impossible to predict.

"How do kickers practice?"

Outside of kicking-and-covering exercises with the entire team, kickers do individual drills and special weight lifting. Sometimes a team's punter may also hold for field goal and extra points because he has the skill and time to work on it. He may even be the backup placekicker so the two can switch roles in practicing.

With the placekicker doing the snapping, the punter may practice fielding poor center snaps or kicking from his own end zone, without benefit of the usual 15-yard distances from scrimmage. If a team runs a fake-punt that involves a pass, the punter can practice this with his placekicker as a receiver.

Punters and place kickers also share the same sense of isolation specialists can feel in a team game. Often, their personalities are the same or compliment each other as they prepare for a job that largely goes unnoticed — until something bad happens. In that case, they are prepared to commiserate in what every team playing the game has: a kicker's support group.

"What's a 'coffin corner' kick?"

The coffin corner is either corner of the playing field, just in front of the end zone, from roughly the goal line to the 5-yard line. The punter tries to place the ball so it lands out of bounds or is downed as close to the end zone as possible, thus forcing the opposition to drive almost the length of the field in an effort to score. A perfect coffin corner kick is one that goes out of bounds inside the one-yard line.

Some people wrongly think the "coffin corner" is named because, when the punt is executed well, the offense is essentially "dead" — with its back to the proverbial wall. Instead, the "coffin corner" kick was named after a decorative, very small corner, cut into the wall of a staircase landing in an old Victorian house — called, of course, the coffin corner.

The coffin corner punt takes much skill; if the kick is too far and into the end zone, the result is a touchback. The ball is then placed on the 20-yard line, a much more favorable position for the receiving team than having to start inside the 5.

"What kind of blocking is used for protecting the punter?"

Teams will use either zone or man-to-man blocking schemes. With zone blocking, the blocker is responsible for a particular area, or gap, regardless of how many rushers try to run through it. It's important in zone schemes that players take tight splits that are closer to each other than in other blocking schemes so teams can't rush more than one man through a gap.

There is some advantage to zone blocking as it can handle punt block schemes the punting team may not have seen before. To attack zone blocking, opponents will try to overload such a zone with multiple rushers, forcing the punter's personal protector(s) to step up and block. At the same time, an outside rusher comes hard and, with a clear path to the kicker, aims at the tail of the protector in anticipation of where the ball will come off the punter's foot. Teams that zone protect usually cover kicks a bit slower than those that block man-to-man.

Man-to-man blocking may afford faster coverage downfield because blockers are immediately released from blocking responsibilities if the man over them does not rush, is lined up deeper than 2 to 3 yards or drops back to block on the snap of the ball.

The blockers will need to be able to switch blocking responsibilities when their man twists or crosses with another rusher, just as offensive linemen need to switch when pass rushers try to crisscross and, in the confusion, break a rusher free to the ball.

"What does a coach tell his players about running down under the punt?"

Players covering the kick are assigned lanes, just as those who cover kickoffs. If a coverage player has to get out of his lane to get away from someone trying to block him, the player next to him has to see this and adjust to maintain the coverage. Those covering need to see the return man and adjust their lanes, converging as they near the returner as well as catching a glimpse of where the ball is coming down. The outside cover men have the best opportunity to see where the ball is because they don't have blockers on both sides of them and can better afford to look up without getting blocked while doing it.

Coaching Points

If, after a short punt, the ball goes out of bounds near midfield, the offense can be much more aggressive with its play calling than if it is pinned near its own end zone because it's not in danger of a safety or a fumble near the goal line.

A punter's attempt to pin the receiving team deep, however, is difficult. The landing area is small, the ball can bounce all sorts of directions once it lands and the kick must be executed in a split-second with rushers bearing down on the punter.

As punters have become more adept at kicking the ball with "English" upon landing, many teams have moved away from coffin corner kicks. Instead, they favor kicking the ball short of the goal line with hopes their players can down it before it reaches the end zone.

Coaches study opponents' game film to find tendencies with their punt formations. If a team shows the same look every time, coaches might create a fake punt play. The run is usually preferable because passes, which can be dropped or intercepted, are a higher risk.

Punt Coverage

Coaches spend lots of time getting their punt coverage team to find the ball and be aware of any player making a fair-catch signal, which prevents anybody on the return team from returning the football once they've caught it. It's absolutely vital that those covering the punt "break down" — go slower — as they get within five yards of the return man, to better help them be under control for a tackle. If you watch punt returns that are broken for long yardage, it's usually because a defender goes out of his lane, the cover men don't break down early enough or the would-be tacklers get caught straight-legged or with their legs crossed.

Blocked Punts

Coaches absolutely hate it when a punt gets blocked because, with film and scouting, every opponent left on the schedule will believe it, too, can block one. Besides having to work extra hard on solving the breakdown that led to the blocked punt, coaches will usually devise a fake punt in an effort to keep the defense off balance.

Fake Punts

It takes courage to call for a fake punt: first, because if the trick fails it often affords the other team great field position; and, second, because it's downright embarrassing to try a fake that doesn't work. However, a successful fake punt play can also provide the momentum an underdog needs to get back in the game and perhaps pull off an upset. It also sends a message to future teams: you'll have to spend practice and coaching time to prepare for our fake. That's why good coaches try a fake punt early in the season: it can discourage punt rushes and cause opponents to spend time on something they wouldn't have otherwise worked on, which means less time for something else.

12.

Punt Returns

I'd catch a punt naked, in the snow, in Buffalo, for a chance to play in the NFL.

— Steve Henderson, NFL hopeful

When a defense stops an offense from getting a first down and forces the opponent to punt, it has an opportunity to earn back big yardage with a good "return."

The punt return can be one of the most exciting plays in football and often can turn a game around — for the receiving team, which might return the punt for a touchdown, or for the kicking team, which might pounce on a botched attempt by the punt returner to catch the ball.

Winning teams usually have a specialist to run back punts who has speed and open-field running ability to avoid tacklers. But the most important skill to have is the ability to catch the ball despite opposing players running full speed at him and the wind sometimes playing havoc with the ball. The returner must also have good judgment, knowing when to signal for a fair catch or let a kick bounce out of bounds or into the end zone.

The first thing a punt-return team must do is make sure the other team actually kicks the ball and doesn't try a fake. Coaches are responsible for lining their return team up in a formation that won't invite a fake and then having one or more players rush the kicker to make sure he punts the ball.

"How do teams block for a punt return?"

Blocking below the waist is not allowed, so blockers must stay on their feet. Because the pursuing players are running, the blockers must run with them — like defensive backs playing bump and run pass coverage against wide receivers. The blocker should establish a position of leverage on his man — slightly ahead — and stay with him.

As the defender slows down or turns towards the return man, the blocker should either shield his man from the returner with his body or push him from the side or front. The cardinal rule is to never block from behind the defender; that's a 10-yard penalty from the spot of the foul. If a blocker leaves his feet and blocks a defender from behind, it's an even more serious penalty for clipping: 15 yards from the spot of the foul.

"The man who complains about the way the ball bounces is likely the one who dropped it."
— **Lou Holtz, coach, Notre Dame**

Sometimes, blockers will not run with the opposing players, but will instead sprint down field to set up a wall return along the sideline. This type of return works well against young, eager or undisciplined defenders who focus totally on the ball and lose sight of where the blockers are going.

By the time the opposing players move to pursue the return man, they have lost leverage on the ball and find themselves pinned in by the blockers in the wall. This return takes a bit more time to set up; it's important that the kick be long so the coverage players get sucked into the trap.

The most effective return can be a middle return, where the blockers take an inside angle on their man and shield them towards the sideline on either side of the formation. The return man needs to immediately head up the field; no time for a lot of moves. In such cases, the blockers need to run and shield the cover players; no need to use their hands and risk a penalty.

Invariably, if you watch a replay of a big return up the middle, the coverage players have left a lane open or run so fast that they couldn't slow down in time to corral the return man. You will also note the number of coverage players who, instead of breaking down with a bend in their knees, are stiff legged and unable to get their body in position to tackle. Getting your legs crossed while trying to make a tackle is a recipe for disaster as well.

Coaching Points

A good punt return depends on, first, a good punt and, second, the return team's blockers getting a leveraged position on their man and maintaining that for 30 to 40 yards down the field. The blockers must be disciplined about hand position and use good judgment when their man turns unexpectedly. Because the covering team has some of its fastest and best athletes covering the kick, this is a steep challenge; witness the number of penalties called on punt returns. Coaches teach their blockers to lift both hands in the air when their man has made a sudden change in direction to show the officials they did not push him in the back.

When a team is pinned deep in its own territory, most coaches tell their return man to stand at the 10-yard-line and let anything beyond him go, with hopes the ball will bound into the end zone and give the team the ball on the 20-yard-line. However, with punters becoming more adept at punting balls that spin backwards, punt returners increasingly will call fair catches even inside their own 5-yard line.

13.

Defense: The Line

Offense sells tickets, defense wins championships.

— **Bear Bryant, coach, Alabama**

The defense is the team that begins a play from scrimmage not in possession of the ball, opposing the offensive team. The objective of the defensive team is to prevent the other team from scoring.

The defense can stop the offense in one of five ways:

(1) by forcing the offense to punt, after the "O" has been unable to move the ball the requisite 10 yards in three plays for a "first down";

(2) by stopping the offensive team "on downs" by preventing it from moving the ball the requisite 10 yards even when it gambles and, instead of punting, "goes for it" on fourth down;

(3) by forcing a fumble that the defense recovers;

(4) by intercepting a pass thrown by the offense;

(5) by preventing the offense from scoring as time expires to end the first or second half of play.

Unlike the offensive team, the rules do not restrict the defensive team into certain positions or specific numbered jerseys. A defensive player may line up anywhere on his side of the line of scrimmage, be moving at the snap of the ball and perform any legal action, including catching — intercepting — forward passes.

Over time, however, defensive roles have become defined into three main sets of players, and several individual positions: the defensive line, linebackers and defensive backs, each of which deserves its own chapter.

Defensive line

These players — usually three or four of them — spread out along the line of scrimmage, close to the ball. They may be in a three-point stance (one hand on the ground) or two-point stance (standing).

Two positions comprise the defensive line: defensive tackles and defensive ends. The tackle is also called a nose guard when he plays directly over the offensive center.

There are usually two tackles in every defense and their primary responsibilities are to stop the run in the middle of the formation and rush the quarterback when he passes. The tackles may be the biggest of the defensive line as they must be strong and able to stand up against two or more offensive linemen attempting to block them.

> *"If you're mad at your kid, you can either raise him to be a nose tackle or send him out to play in the freeway. It's about the same."*
> — **Bob Golic, NFL lineman**

The two defensive ends line up outside the defensive tackles, at the edges of the defensive line. Their responsibilities are more complicated than the tackles' and, thus, require more athleticism and speed.

Defensive ends have two important jobs: rush the passer and establish "contain" on runs that are aimed outside the middle defense, preventing, if possible, the ball carrier running outside the end. The faster of the two is usually placed on the right side of the defensive line (quarterback's left) because that's a right-handed quarterback's blind side. Defensive ends often start in two-point stances to better see the quarterback and key the ball quickly, plus their friends and family — wink, wink — can see them better from the stands.

Two kinds of defensive fronts are used in football: odd-man fronts and even-man fronts. You can tell the difference by looking at the center. If he is "covered" — has a defender aligned on him — the defensive line is termed an odd front. The defender over the center is called a "nose guard" because he is aligned on the center's nose.

The line is called an even front when the center is uncovered, in which case the guards on either side of the center may be covered by defenders. Usually the defensive linemen aligned on offensive linemen are down in three-point stances, although you may occasionally see teams have their defensive linemen standing up to better read the quarterback, usually in passing situations, or to create confusion with the offensive linemen's ability to figure out who they should block.

"What is the difference between a one-gap and two-gap defense?"

The one-gap system is a defense most coaches believe in wholeheartedly when they want to simplify reactions and assignments for their players. Former NFL Coach Jon Gruden says, "You have four linemen, you get the hat in the crack (gap in the offensive line) and penetrate, disrupt, as opposed to a two-gap, '34' type of approach where you have three linemen and there is more reading and reacting."

One-gap defense: A one-gap defense is mainly found in a 4-3 front where each defensive lineman has a one-gap responsibility. He is aggressive on the snap of the ball, penetrating that hole and then "owning" the gap he's assigned.

He's expected to tackle any running back headed his way, or to force the running back to cut back toward a teammate. If the play is a pass, the defender should rush the quarterback through his gap. A one-gap defensive linemen's task is to take on his man and occupy that space.

Two-gap defense: In this scheme, a defensive lineman is responsible for both the A and B gaps — inside and outside — on his side of the ball. In this way, three defensive linemen can defend six gaps, tying up blockers from getting to the inside linebackers. The lineman's initial reaction must be to read the offense's first movement and anticipate which gap a running back is heading for, step into that gap and "own it." A two-gap defensive lineman generally has more area to defend and is expected to take blockers head on and defend the gaps on either side of his shoulders; this requires more discipline.

"Why choose a one-gap defense?"

If a coach has smaller defensive linemen who are quick and good pass rushers, he might choose a one-gap defense. One-gap defensive schemes lend themselves to blitzing and long-yardage passing situations with lots of options for the defensive coaches.

To defend the wide-open passing offenses today, a one-gap scheme is more effective at getting pressure on the quarterback, getting more sacks and tackles than two-gap linemen.

"Why run a two-gap defense"?

When executing well, a two-gap defensive lineman is able to fill between two offensive linemen, plugging two gaps. If a coach has mostly big, slower defensive linemen who struggle with pass rushing, he might choose to run a two-gap defense. The linemen in a two-gap defense must be satisfied with the tedious task of distracting and occupying the offensive blockers while the linebackers get all the glory. If up against a power running offense, a two-gap defense may be more effective at stopping the run.

Pass Rushing

Good pass defense begins at the line of scrimmage and defensive linemen are important in getting pressure on the quarterback: sacking him for a loss, disrupting his vision and focus, or forcing him into hurried, inaccurate throws; all this helps the "back-end" defenders — linebackers and defensive backs — who are scrambling to cover pass receivers behind them.

"You got one guy going boom, one guy going whack, and one guy not getting into the end zone."

— John Madden, coach, Oakland Raiders

It helps to be tall, but even shorter defensive linemen can get their hands up when they rush, or when they are stalemated by an offensive lineman pass blocking. A tipped pass often results in an interception and, at the least, frustrates quarterbacks who had players open down the field and frustrates receivers anxious to get the ball.

Defenders must rush the passer cautiously; watch to see if they rush deeper than the quarterback's depth, thus giving him the opportunity to "keep and run." In such cases, he can step up inside his own tackles and run free outside because the defensive ends are too

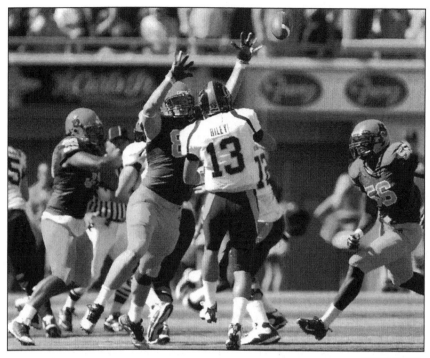

Jerry Thompson

Two defenders unable to sack the quarterback get their hands up to obscure his vision and disrupt his timing. It is an overlooked form of intimidation that can destroy the confidence and accuracy of even the best signal callers.

deep to come back and tackle him. The outside rusher also can't go inside the offensive tackle unless some other player is covering the flank for him; otherwise, the quarterback can simply run to that side because there's no "contain." Discipline must kick in. The defensive end has to resist his ego — get a sack at any cost — and maintain his pass rush responsibility.

Watch the hands of the offensive and defensive linemen of both teams in a passing situation. The offense is trying to "punch" the defenders' chests, stopping their momentum and then pushing them away, maintaining a pocket for the quarterback to see the field and quickly throw a pass.

The defensive linemen also use their hands to keep the offensive linemen's hands off them, trying to push blockers off balance so they can cut a path to the passer.

One of the top rushers in the NFL has his own martial arts coach who has taught him hand moves that break down the hands of the blocker trying to hold him up. Most great teams have players on both sides of the ball who have learned to use their hands quickly and powerfully.

The defensive lineman (right) attempts to get the blocker's hands away from his chest. Both have set their feet solidly and the defender has a slight advantage with leverage.

Causing Fumbles

Excellent defensive teams are opportunistic at causing fumbles. Every team works on this; defenders know ball carriers need to carry the ball "high and tight," with one hand over the tip, against the chest. When in traffic, the carrier is supposed to get his other hand over the other tip to protect it.

A defensive rule of thumb suggests if one tackler has the ball carrier held up, the others come in to rip the ball out. It's called "gang tackling." The method for ripping the ball out is to get your hand on the opposite end of the football that the ball carrier is clutching. The ball is oblong and has rounded edges, and if you can get your hand on the tip and pull hard, it doesn't matter how tightly the carrier is grasping it, the football is going to come out. That's why you see secondary tacklers, when they gang up on the runner, pulling as if they're trying to start a lawn mower.

14.

Defense:
The Linebackers

I like linebackers. I collect them. You can't have too many good ones.

— **Bill Parcells, coach, Dallas Cowboys**

Defenses will have two to four players lined up behind the defensive line in two-point stances — standing. Linebackers are bigger than defensive backs and smaller than defensive linemen. They're a blend of the strength of defensive linemen and the speed and quickness of defensive backs. Linebackers must be physically tough and radiate the desire to make as many tackles as possible; tackling is an absolute must for a good rush defense.

In early football, linebackers were big, physical and slow. With wide-open spread offenses today, linebackers need to be quick and athletic to defend option runs and pass routes in their defensive zones.

Linebackers need to quickly recognize the difference between a run play and a pass play; in the event of a pass, they drop and cover receivers in the open field. Opposing coaches will watch their every move on video and look for weaknesses in their run or pass coverage.

Sometimes, linebackers who react too fast to run fakes will get sucked in on a play-action pass, when the quarterback fakes a handoff and throws a pass. Good linebackers have an instinctual feel for knowing the difference. Bad ones don't. As they say, there's a sucker born every minute.

"Which player organizes the defense on the field?"

If the quarterback is the leader of the offense, the middle linebacker is the leader of the defense. He often gets the defensive signals from the coaches and relays those to the rest of the team.

In a 4-3 defense there is one middle — inside — linebacker while in a 3-4 there are two inside and two outside linebackers. In a 3-4, of the two inside linebackers, the one aligned to the tight end side of the offense, is usually the middle linebacker.

A good middle linebacker is often the leading tackler on the defense because of his talent and toughness — and his desire to be around the ball at all times.

Defensive coaches need their linebackers to be versatile tacklers in the open field and inside the tackles on the line of scrimmage where the rough stuff happens.

"What is a strong-side linebacker?"

The strong side of the offensive line is the side on which the tight end lines up — or whichever side of the formation has the most personnel. The strong-side linebacker — the "Sam" — usually lines up head up — across from — the tight end.

He's most often the strongest linebacker; at the very least he must possess the strength and ability to shed blocks from the best blockers on the offense: a tight end or fullback.

The strong-side linebacker is a combination of linebacker and defensive back: he should have the same pass-coverage skills as a strong safety in order to cover the tight end in man-to-man situations. What's more, he must have the quickness to read offensive formations and drop back into coverage in pass situations.

"What is a weak-side linebacker?"

The weak-side linebacker must be the fastest of the three linebackers, because he's often the one called into pass coverage, particularly against slot formations where he may be playing head up on a slot receiver. He's often in pursuit of a play away from his position, so speed and quickness in avoiding blockers is a necessity.

Because of his position on the weak side — opposite the tight end — the "Will" rarely has to face large interior linemen one-on-one unless one is pulling towards him. Offensive coaches will sometimes bring in another tight end to balance the formation and force the defense's weak outside linebacker to line up over the second tight end, creating a physical mismatch and then running the ball directly at him.

Linebackers in 4-3 Defense

There are three linebackers and four down linemen in a 4-3 defense, which is not considered the best alignment against powerful offensive rushing attacks. The middle linebacker is designated "Mike" and the two outside linebackers are called "Sam" and "Will" according to how they line up against the offensive formation. (Coaches name linebackers with a variety of names, but the first letter of each indicates whether they are "strong," "middle" or "weak.")

"Mike" and "Sam" usually line up against what is considered the main rushing side of the offensive formation with "Sam" head up on the tight end. The middle linebacker's responsibility is to stop runs inside the two offensive tackles, see the whole field and get to the ball as quickly as possible.

The outside linebacker's job is to defeat any blockers, contain the outside run and rush the quarterback or drop back in coverage against a pass.

"I like football. I find it's an exciting, strategic game. It's a great way to avoid conversation with your family at Thanksgiving."
— Craig Ferguson, TV show host

On pass plays, the linebackers' responsibilities vary based on whether man-to-man or zone coverage has been called. In zone coverage, the linebackers will generally drop into "hook" zones, the short- and mid-range areas eight to 12 yards deep. To do so, they divide their coverage responsibilities into quarters, with a defensive back taking one of the four.

A defensive back usually has the other short-quarter area. In some defensive coverages, one or both the outside linebackers may spread wider into the flat outside the hash marks, eight to 12 yards deep.

In a man-to-man coverage the "Sam" will often cover the tight end with help on deep passes from a safety; at other times, the "Will" and "Sam" will be responsible for the first man out of the backfield on their side of the center, with the "Mike" covering if a second back slips out of the backfield on that side of the field.

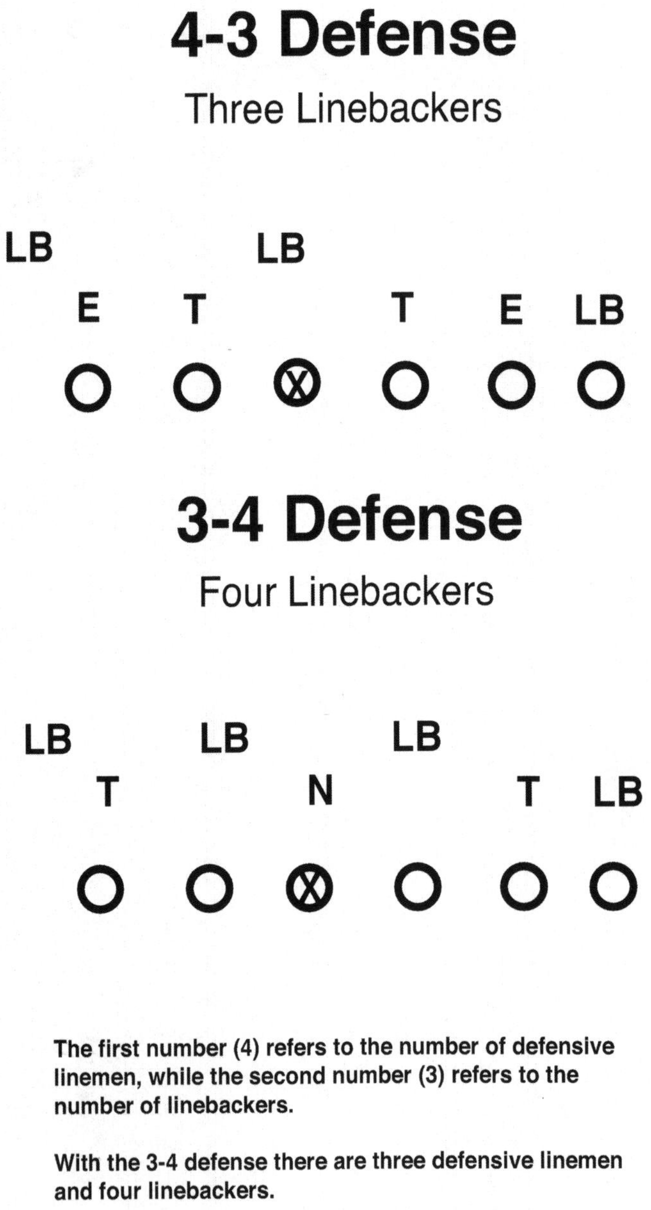

4-3 Defense

Three Linebackers

LB   LB

E   T   T   E   LB

O   O   ⊗   O   O   O

3-4 Defense

Four Linebackers

LB   LB   LB

T   N   T   LB

O   O   ⊗   O   O   O

The first number (4) refers to the number of defensive linemen, while the second number (3) refers to the number of linebackers.

With the 3-4 defense there are three defensive linemen and four linebackers.

Diagram 6. 4-3 and 3-4 defenses.

Offensive coaches will try to get a third receiver out of the backfield and up the sideline when they feel he has a speed advantage over the middle linebacker. This often happens on the goal line or blitz situations.

Most often, the offense will challenge the weak linebacker man-to-man because he is in man coverage more than "Mike."

Linebackers in 3-4 Defense

In the 3–4 alignment, three linemen play the line of scrimmage with four linebackers backing them up: two inside linebackers and two outside. The idea behind the 3–4 defense is to disguise where the fourth rusher will come from; coaches love this element of the defense. Instead of the four down-linemen in the 4–3, only three defenders are attacking on nearly every play.

The defense depends on three large linemen who must be double-teamed, especially the nose guard, who plays over the offensive center. By holding his ground and forcing two offensive linemen to block him, the nose guard protects the inside linebackers so they're free to run to the ball and make tackles.

Because the inside linebackers line up over the offensive guards, the nose guard must occupy both the center and one of the guards to keep the linebacker free of an immediate blocking threat on the snap of the ball.

There are two key fundamentals for linebackers: take on blockers with their inside shoulder (the shoulder nearest to where the ball was snapped) and keep their outside arm (closest to the sideline) free. All defenses are based on leverage and forcing the ball to cut back inside to where most of the defensive players are coming from; these are critical skills every defender on a great defensive team displays.

If a linebacker hits with his outside shoulder, he automatically loses leverage and gives the offense a chance to run around him, outside, where the big yardage is. The same goes if the linebacker can't keep his outside arm free of the blocker, in which case he loses leverage and the inside-run defense is breached. When you watch a replay of a big gain on a running play, look for the defenders who hit with the wrong shoulder and can't keep their outside arm free. That's how you beat a defense.

"What if the linebackers aren't good pass defenders?"

In long-yardage or passing situations, coaches will substitute defensive backs for slower defensive ends or linebackers when they want their best pass defenders on the field. Watch for these situations (easier to check those players leaving than those coming on the field) and see if the defense plays man or zone pass defense; it might mean they're going to blitz and don't want slow defenders trying to cover fast receivers.

At other times, defensive coaches want to have enough fast defenders to match up with spread offenses that might have five receivers lined up; there's not much need for linebackers when there are no running backs on the field.

"What are the average sizes of college defensive football players?"

Defensive ends: 6-4, 253 pounds.
Defensive tackles: 6-2, 281 pounds.
Linebackers: 6-2, 226 pounds.
Safeties: 6-0, 200 pounds.
Corner backs: 5-11, 183 pounds.

As with offensive players, high school defensive players' size and speed vary; youngsters are not yet mature physically and have a lot of room left to grow.

Professional players are bigger, stronger, faster and more athletic than college defensive players. As a general rule, pro defensive linemen are much more athletic than professional offensive linemen. Defensive backs are also equal to the top athletes who play offense.

15.

Blitzes and Defensive Backs

Most football players are temperamental. That's 90% temper and 10% mental.

— **Doug Plank, NFL player**

A normal pass rush consists of any four defenders coming at the quarterback; a blitz is bringing five or more rushers. By nature, blitzes are risky for the defense, taking away pass coverage defenders to rush the quarterback. If the secondary misses an assignment, a big gain or score can result. The defense often does not — and cannot — cover all offensive players, but blitzing is forcefully pressuring the quarterback in an attempt to sack him, throw off his timing or force him to fumble or throw an interception.

A blitz doesn't necessarily have to end with a sack. The pressure the quarterback sees and feels from a blitz, even if his blockers pick up all the rushers, can cause him to lose his timing and poise. If the quarterback's head is moving quickly from side to side when he's looking for receivers, he's rattled and the defense gets the upper hand.

The most common blitzes are linebacker blitzes. There are also safety blitzes — usually the strong safety — and corner blitzes, where a cornerback comes from the short side of the field. These are less common because sending a defensive back on a blitz is even riskier than a linebacker in that it removes a primary pass defender from coverage. However, well-timed

Stunts

Executed by defensive linemen

Left side of diagram: Defensive tackle goes first, driving through outside shoulder of the offensive guard. The defensive end loops inside and behind his defensive tackle, who now must contain outside.

Right side of diagram: Defensive end slants first through inside shoulder of offensive tackle. Defensive tackle loops behind defensive end to contain outside.

Stunts are used to confuse the blocking assignments of the offensive line in passing situations against man or zone blocking schemes where they must block anyone coming in their gap.

One rusher goes first, forcing his blocker to go with him. The other takes a step to hold the blocker's attention and create a gap for his teammate while he circles behind.

If executed properly there is a good chance the offensive linemen will get tangled up, leaving one of the rushers free.

Diagram 7. Stunts.

Blitz
Executed by linebackers

Five or more rush, including linebackers attempting to overload one side of the offensive formation with more rushers than there are blockers to stop them

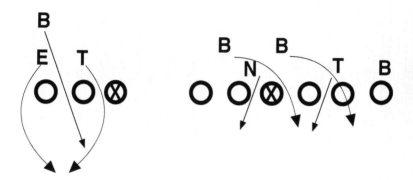

Blitz
Including strong safety

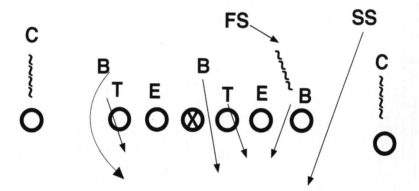

Diagram 8. Blitzes

Jerry Thompson

The proper position for a shoulder tackle: head up, legs working underneath, arms wrapping, and driving the runner backwards.

pressure can be overwhelming to the offense because of the surprise factor; the offensive team's blockers are rarely ready to meet the onslaught.

The defense might try to "overload" one side of the offensive line — say, sending four rushers from a split formation when only a guard, tackle and perhaps a back is in position to block for the quarterback. The coach is gambling that his defense can get the quarterback before Mr. QB can spot an open receiver — or at least force him out of the pocket. To get a sack is ideal, but, again, blitz pressure is effective in forcing a QB out of his comfort zone and into mistakes, particularly as the game deepens and he keeps feeling the heat.

"What is a zone blitz?"

The zone blitz is designed to confuse the offensive line and quarterback by having defenders lined up to rush the passer before the snap and unexpectedly retreat, into zone pass coverage, when the ball is snapped. And, at the same time, surprise the passer by rushing one or more defenders who had originally positioned to "cover" the receivers before the snap.

This is a timed blitz, a split-second after the snap of the ball, ideally giving the offense no time to react and adjust; thus, it can result in player mismatches that leave gaps in the pass protection. This gives the unexpected rushers a clear and quick path to tackling the passer before he has time to throw to an open receiver. If done at the right time, the quarterback may try to throw a hot route to a receiver away from the blitz and throw it directly to a defender who is normally rushing him and is now, surprisingly, dropping back as a pass defender.

This blitz works well against inexperienced quarterbacks because they are confronted with something they can't anticipate. A possible problem for the defense? If the offensive line adjusts its blocking assignments after the snap, the protection holds up and the experienced quarterback can throw a short pass to an uncovered receiver. With five or more rushers and the rest of the defenders playing zone, the defense can't cover all the zones on both sides of the field. Thus, a zone blitz can be a scary call by the defensive coordinator.

Live By the Blitz, Die By the Blitz

A blitz is a gamble for a defense because the secondary must play man-to-man pass defense on all eligible receivers — up to five in a spread formation. The offense could match up their fastest receiver against the slowest defensive back, who would have no help.

Many safeties are not the best cover defenders; against blitz-oriented teams, look for teams to run post routes — patterns in which the receiver slants toward the middle of the field, where the goal posts are — and corner routes — long patterns in which the receiver breaks outside to end zone pylons— to exploit the safeties.

During blitzes, offenses can also hurt defenses if the QB runs an option because all the defensive backs are chasing pass receivers, leaving the front defenders with no help if they miss a tackle. This is why defensive coaches say their worst nightmare is a passing team that can also run an option.

Defensive Backs

Defensive backs make up what's called the secondary, usually four players lined up behind the defensive line and linebackers. Most defenses have four defensive backs, but some run-oriented defenses may have only three. Defensive backs are primarily used to defend pass plays by covering wide receivers and tight ends, with hopes of intercepting passes or preventing receivers from otherwise catching the ball.

Defensive backs need to be excellent tacklers in the open field as they are the last line of defense beyond the defensive line and linebackers. In long-yardage passing situations, teams will often put in a fifth defender — called a nickel back — and even a sixth — dime defender — to better defend.

Defensive backs are the smallest defenders on the field and the fastest because they must cover the offense's often-fast wide receivers on pass routes. There are usually two corners — one on each side of the formation — whose main strength is pass coverage, and two safeties: a "free" safety and a "strong" safety.

The free safety plays the middle of the field, deep, and works to help the corners on long pass plays down the sideline. The free safety also rushes up to help support the line and linebackers on runs. The strong safety is a combination of defensive back and linebacker. He may line up at the same depth as the linebackers — five to seven yards — and, unlike the free safety, his initial responsibility is run defense.

Defensive backs can jam and push receivers downfield as long as the receiver is in front of them and a threat to block on running plays. Once a pass has been thrown or the receiver runs past the defensive back, he can't put his hands on the receiver. This college rule is different from the pro rule, which allows defensive backs to use their hands only on receivers no more than five yards beyond the line of scrimmage.

Defensive back coaches use an array of formations and cover patterns, but they must be careful to coordinate it with the correct run defense lest, on a blitz, for example, huge areas of the field are left uncovered and might be exploited by the offense.

"What are the basic pass coverages?"

Man: Straight man-to-man coverage with no help from safeties who are busy covering an offensive receiver or a running back man-to-man themselves. This defense may be used when a blitz has been called, though it's risky against a good passing team with fast receivers.

Man Free: Man-to-man coverage with a safety not assigned a player to cover —"free" — and, instead, supports other defensive backs on deep pass routes. Coaches need talented and fast defensive backs to run this coverage, especially with the variety of formations offensive teams have at their disposal.

Cover two: Two-deep zone coverage with the safeties lined up on the hash marks about 12 to 15 yards beyond the line of scrimmage,

Pass Coverage

Cover 1

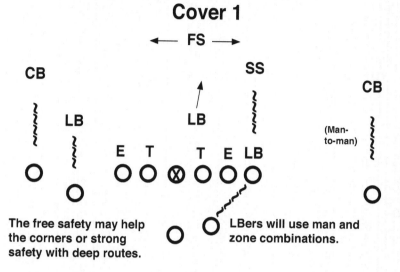

The free safety may help the corners or strong safety with deep routes.

LBers will use man and zone combinations.

Cover 2

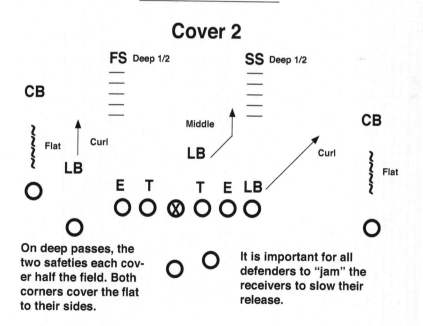

On deep passes, the two safeties each cover half the field. Both corners cover the flat to their sides.

It is important for all defenders to "jam" the receivers to slow their release.

Diagram 9. Cover 1 and Cover 2 pass coverages.

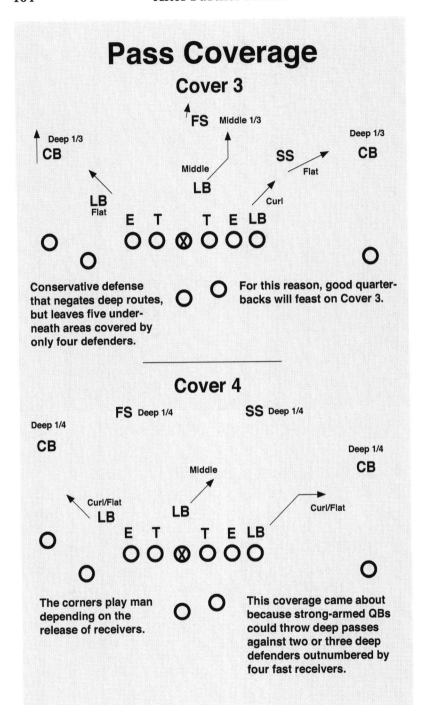

Pass Coverage

Cover 3

Conservative defense that negates deep routes, but leaves five underneath areas covered by only four defenders.

For this reason, good quarterbacks will feast on Cover 3.

Cover 4

The corners play man depending on the release of receivers.

This coverage came about because strong-armed QBs could throw deep passes against two or three deep defenders outnumbered by four fast receivers.

Diagram 10. Cover 3 and Cover 4 pass coverages.

each covering half the field. There are five "underneath" defenders: the cornerbacks cover a flat zone on each side of the field, from the hash mark to the sideline, 7-15 yards deep. The outside linebackers cover the hook zones. Finally, a middle linebacker covers the middle curl zone at about the same depth as the corners.

> ## "I make my practices real hard because if a player is a quitter, I want him to quit in practice not in a game."
> —*Bear Bryant, Alabama coach*

Offenses will attack this coverage down the sidelines, behind the corner, before the safety can arrive to prevent the catch and straight down the middle of the field, splitting the two safeties. The receiver splitting the safeties is usually a tight end or slot back who must beat the short coverage of a linebacker who is trying to run with him down the middle. The corners must "jam" (jolt, push) the outside receivers as they release down the field to slow them down and to disrupt their timing with the quarterback. Receivers don't like two-deep defenses because getting roughed up by a defensive back throws off their timing with the quarterback.

Defenses can also run a "cover two man," where every receiver is covered by a defensive player in man-to-man coverage, with the two safeties playing the deep zones.

Defenses will often bring in one or more extra defensive backs to replace linebackers or lineman for better pass coverage.

Cover three: Frequently called zone coverage with the strong safety playing the flat — from the hash marks to the sideline, 8 to 15 yards deep. Both cornerbacks guard the deep third and the free safety plays deep middle.

Cover four: Referred to as "quarters," with the corners and safeties dropping into deep coverage, each taking one-fourth the width of the field.

"How do teams cover passes on the goal line?"

There is a running argument between secondary coaches about the alignment a cornerback should take against a receiver in goal line man-to-man situations.

One theory, the older one, is that the defensive back should align on the inside eye, or shoulder, of the receiver. From there, the defensive back

Pick Play Defense
Against 'man' coverage

Outside corner jams re-
lease of end and cuts off
post route. Inside corner
goes around, or in front
of, his mate to cover the
flat route of the slot. Both
defenders must avoid
contact with receivers
attempting to pick them.

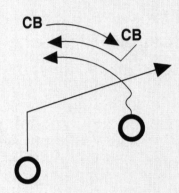

Against 'zone' coverage

Each corner reads the
release of the two receivers. The outside corner
will take the receiver
going to the flat and the
inside corner will pick up
the inside route, like a
"switch" in basketball.

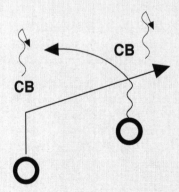

Diagram 11. Pick play

denies the receiver a quick release, such as on a post route, where there is no one else to help him. The defender is in position to jolt the receiver if he tries to go inside and if he releases outside, the defensive back runs with the receiver, maintaining the inside angle. By forcing the receiver outside, towards the sideline, he is cutting down the chance of easy throws for the quarterback.

> ## "Football is not a body contact game. Dancing is a body contact game, football is a collision game."
> — **Duffy Daugherty, coach, Michigan State**

To offset this coverage, quarterbacks will throw a "back-shoulder fade" which is a pass thrown at the outside shoulder of the receiver, slightly underthrown, so the defender can never see where the ball is going. The pass often ends up looking like a basketball jump ball in which one player rebounds the ball over the top of the other.

Not surprisingly, many excellent pass receivers were also good basketball players in high school.

The other alignment is "head up" but from here, the receiver has two ways to go — quickly. If he fakes outside, and the defensive back spreads his legs or turns, the receiver goes the other way inside for an easy score on a high-percentage pass. If the receiver fakes inside, causing the defender to give ground or turn his feet, the receiver can gain separation for an easy touchdown on a fade route.

Secondary coaches believe that in a head-up position the corner can see the receiver and ball better. That said, rookie corners without a lot of playing experience can struggle with that alignment.

As a spectator, find out the experience of each team's corners and watch how they play the goal line.

"What is a 'pick play' and when is it used?"

A "pick play" (Diagram 11) occurs when two receivers cross their routes, forcing one of the defenders covering to have to run around — preferably, for the offense's sake, *behind* — the other receiver to catch up to the man he's covering. You see this a lot near the goal line because the defense relies more on tight man-to-man coverage in that area; it's like basketball when a pick is set and both defenders get caught up with one player while the other breaks free.

However, unlike basketball picks, which are legal, in football they are illegal — supposedly. Sophisticated pass offenses will do this anywhere on the field to open up zones and receivers who are working together. Receivers are coached to avoid contact with the defensive backs but disrupt them by getting in their way. An offensive pass interference penalty occurs if the receiver runs into the defender but it's not a penalty if the defensive back runs into another defender while trying to cover a receiver.

"How do you defend a pick play?"

Defenses can give up touchdowns on pick plays where the receivers cross and the defenders collide while trying to cover the inside receiver. The best way to cover is "bracket" coverage, where the outside defender waits and picks up the widest receiver, turning over the inside-breaking receiver to his inside defender. It's like a "switch" in basketball.

The other way is for the defender to fight through the pick and stay with his man; it takes an exceptionally disciplined back, usually a pro, to pull this off. Watch for the pick plays; offenses will often try this in a goal-line or a short-yardage situation in which they anticipate man-to-man coverage.

16.

The Line of Scrimmage

As concerning football, I protest unto you that it may rather be called a friendly kind of fight than a play or recreation — a bloody and murthering practise than a fellowly sport or pastime. And hereof groweth envy, malice, rancour, choler, hatred, displeasure, enmity and what not else; and sometimes fighting, brawling, contention, quarrel-picking, murder, homicide and great effusion of blood, as experience daily teacheth.

— Philip Stubbes, English pamphleteer, 1583

The game is fought hand-to-hand along the line of scrimmage, the one-yard neutral zone between the offensive and defensive linemen. Many fans miss some of the most interesting action of the game because they're busy watching the players run, throw, catch and kick the ball; they miss the coordinated ballet of muscle that explodes each play in what is commonly referred to as the "pit." (OK, so it's "rough" ballet; nevertheless, there's a rhythm and beauty to it.)

"How do defensive linemen know where to line up and what to do?"

A defensive lineman has to have a road map telling him where to line up and what his responsibility is because defenders move their positions

Technique

Where Each Defender Lines Up
to Defend His Assigned Gap

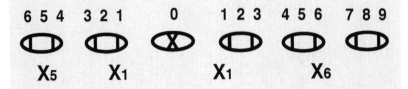

Linebackers have techniques as well, but they're even more complicated

---

Gaps

Area of Responsibility
for Each Defender

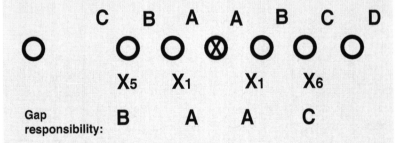

Linebackers have
C, B and D gaps

Diagram 12. Defensive techniques and gaps.

more than offensive linemen. For example, an offensive guard is always going to line up between the center and the tackle. For the defensive linemen, the line of scrimmage consists of two elements: where they line up and what their responsibility is. Defensive linemen never line up the same way play after play, so they have numbers — and different techniques — to help them determine where to line up (Diagram 12).

A zero technique is head up on the center, a one technique on the inside shoulder of the guard, a two technique head up on the guard and a three technique on the outside shoulder of the guard and so on, all the way to outside a tight end, which would be the nine technique. A defensive tackle will line up three different ways on the guard: head up (2 technique); inside shoulder of the guard (1 technique); or outside shoulder of the guard (3 technique).

Once the defensive lineman lines up, he needs to know his basic responsibility and for this, coaches designate the gaps between offensive linemen using letters. The gap between the center and guard on both sides is the A gap, the gap between the guard and tackle on both sides is the B gap and the gap between the tackle and tight end on both sides is the C gap. So it follows that a defensive tackle could be lined up in a two or one technique, responsible for defending the A gap.

A defensive tackle could also be lined up in a 2-3-4 or 5 technique and be responsible for the B or C gap, depending on the defense. Remember that linebackers, aligned on the second level behind the defensive linemen, are also responsible for alignments and gaps, so it's not all up to the defensive linemen; obviously, linemen must be coordinated with linebackers in order to present a united and organized defense, defending all the gaps.

"How do offensive linemen know what to do?"

The road map for offensive linemen is different; it uses numbers so that the running backs know where the play is directed (Diagram 13). The numbers designate holes, which are even to the right of the center and odd to the left. The 1 hole is between the center and left guard, the 2 hole is between the center and right guard, the 3 hole between the left guard and tackle, the 4 hole between the right guard and tackle, the 5 hole between the left tackle and tight end, and the 6 hole between the tackle and tight end on the right side. The 7 and 8 holes are outside the tight ends on the left and right sides, respectively.

The running backs are numbered also; the quarterback could be 1, the fullback 2 and the running back 3, for example. An off-tackle play to the right with the fullback carrying the ball would be 24 or 26, depending on

Where to Run
Right: Even-Numbered Holes
Left: Odd-Numbered Holes

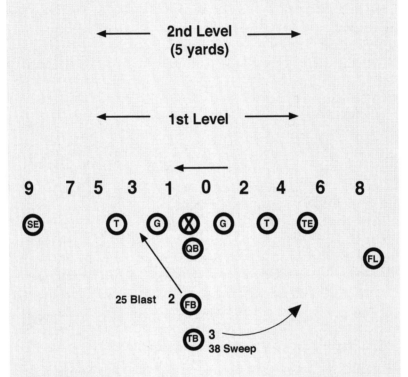

Each back is numbered. If the coach wants his tailback to run around right end, the play would be called "38 sweep" (the three back around the eight hole). If he wants the fullback to run to the left, it might be called "25 blast."

Diagram 13. How holes are usually labeled for runners.

exactly where the coaches want the ball to go. If the running back was the ball carrier on a play designed to go around the end, the play might be called 37 or 38, depending on the direction — right or left — desired by the coaches.

These examples are simplified. The offense is expanded greatly — and grows more complicated — by lining up the backs in multiple formations, giving defensive coaches and players much more to worry about.

"Why does the center point at the opposing players when he gets over the ball?"

Because of no-huddle offenses and different blocking schemes, the linemen need to know the man or area they are to block. When the center points to the defense, he is letting the rest of the linemen know which player he is starting his count with.

The rest of the linemen then count to their individual man, using the center's man as their starting point. In this way, the center acts as a quarterback of the linemen, to the degree that he's also expected to recognize where defensive safeties line up, indicating the type of front the defense is playing.

"How do the offensive linemen know who to block?"

In zone blocking, if an offensive lineman is responsible for the "A gap," at the snap of the ball he steps to that gap and blocks whoever shows up first. If there is a defender there who moves away, the offensive lineman must be alert for another defender coming to that gap.

If no one shows, he continues his path to the "second level" of the defense: the area behind the defensive line occupied by linebackers.

It takes a great deal of skill and athletic ability to do this smoothly because the defenders are not just standing around waiting to be blocked; they are on the move, reading their own individual keys — movement of offensive players — and running to their gap responsibilities.

An effective offensive lineman must be able to recognize and anticipate various defensive adjustments and movements. Every offensive player is also being eyed, or "keyed," by a defender. Each will react to protect his responsibility when that offensive player makes his initial reaction on the snap of the ball.

The offensive player will have to respond to the reaction of the defender to maintain his position of leverage, either knocking his man on his backside or shielding him away from where the ball is being carried or passed.

Coaching Points

Every coach will tell you that winning in football depends on two essentials: stopping the run on defense and running the ball successfully on offense. Do that and your locker room is likely going to be joyful after the game and it's going to be easier for players to find dates. But to accomplish this a team needs to have strong, disciplined players who don't make many mistakes. To win you must dominate your opponent physically where it matters most: the line of scrimmage.

To some it might seem trivial, but lining up correctly is a big deal; a player in the wrong place provides the opponent with an open gap on both offense and defense. Fans love to see their team blitz on defense, with five or more players boring down on the quarterback in schemes designed to overrun the opponent's offense. But there's a risk, too.

Bringing defenders to, or through, a gap leaves the defensive backs thin on help with coverage of receivers. Every offense has the potential of five receivers and, in a blitz situation, every rusher in a gap has to be blocked. If one defender misses the call or covers the wrong receiver or no one at all, an embarrassing gain or touchdown may well be the result.

Because of this, coaches must be wary in deciding when and where to pressure the offense. Most fans, already with a secure mortgage, don't think this through when clamoring for a blitz, totally unaware of the risky nature of bringing defensive pressure. Indeed, risks can ultimately lead to unemployment for coaches.

Offense Initiates, Defense Reacts

Offensive coaches will have their players line up one way before the play and then shift (change) their positions to force the defense to recognize a new formation, move to a different position and remember a different responsibility. Doing this as a steady diet on offense can wear defenders out and cause them to make mental mistakes.

As opposed to offensive coaches, defensive coaches need more practice and meeting time to teach their players to recognize and react to all of the opponent's different formations and personnel groupings. Some defensive coaches will attempt to change with the offense while others simplify by staying in the same defense. Offensive play-callers froth at the mouth when this happens because if they know what the defense will do in certain situations, it gives them a big advantage, like knowing who's going to win before you lay down a bet.

17.

The Battle Begins

Trying to maintain order during a legalized gang brawl involving 80 toughs with a little whistle, a hanky and a ton of prayer.

— **Anonymous referee, explaining his job**

As, historically, battles in war began in the trenches, so does a football game begin on the line of scrimmage, a one-yard neutral zone between the offensive and defensive lines facing each other. Until the ball is snapped by the center to a player in the offensive backfield — usually the quarterback — the neutral zone must be clear of penetration by either side. If a defender crosses into the neutral zone before the snap, a 5-yard penalty is called ("offside"). If an offensive player moves into the neutral zone before the snap the penalty is also 5 yards for what's called "illegal procedure." Offside, illegal shift, illegal motion — all stem from the "illegal procedure" family.

Coaching Point

It's a sign of poor teamwork, concentration, and/or coaching to be penalized for offside or illegal procedure. All players should be watching the ball and restrict their charge until it moves. Obviously, tension, fatigue and crowd noise can disrupt the focus of players on either side.

Jerry Thompson

The defensive lineman (left) is trying to keep the pass blocker's hands away from his chest while the blocker fights to keep the defender's hands away from his. The offensive lineman will be penalized 15 yards for "hands to the face" of the defender.

The offensive players set a snap count in a huddle or on the line of scrimmage by signals. The quarterback calls out the signals or gives a hand or foot signal that the rest of the offensive players can see or hear to determine the snap and their movement. On a verbal count, for example, the QB might say: "Set, hut, hut, hut." The ball is snapped on whichever numbered "hut" the quarterback called in the huddle.

"What does it sound like when the quarterback calls an audible?"

An example would be for the Badgers to have their "live color" as red. If the quarterback shouts "red" it alerts the team the play is being changed. It might go like this: *"Red, 34, red 34!"* Translated, that means the play called in the huddle is changed to 34 and the center is to snap the ball to the quarterback on the standard count for all audibles. It's vital that the offensive players be on the same page or they will embarrass themselves with shoddy execution. It never looks good when half the team moves and the other half just stands there, especially to the alumni and season ticket holders on homecoming.

"What if the other team is catching on to the audibles?"

Quarterbacks might call fake audibles to keep the defense honest. For example, he might yell, *"Green, 34, green 34!,"* meaning "run the original play called."

Sometimes players work out their own "live color." For example, any "hot" color called by the quarterback (red, yellow, orange, pink) could be used to change a play, while a "cool" color (blue, green, black, purple, brown) could be used as the "dummy" call. This is a place where players can have some fun making them up on their own. Anything to keep the defense from knowing for sure what play is coming.

"Is there ever a time you want the other team to think it knows what play is coming from an audible?"

Yes. Let's say Play 34 has been called at the line of scrimmage several times and the defense figures it out. In the huddle, the quarterback calls *"34 play action pass, z bomb, anchor,"* which is a streak pattern by the flanker after a fake of the 34 run play by the quarterback and running back. "Anchor" means to all the offensive players that, *"no matter what color or number I call at the line of scrimmage, we're not changing the play, the one called in the huddle."* As the offense lines up, the quarterback shouts out *"Red, 34, red 34!*" and the defenders all start yelling, *"they're running the ball!"* The ball is snapped and the offensive line, running back and quarterback fake the 34 run play. However, because the defense is expecting — and reacting to what they think is — a run, its defensive backs, in particular, are in no position to cover a pass. For teams caught by surprise like this, the result is, at best, a sizeable gain and, at worst, a touchdown.

"Can defensive players call out their own signals to confuse the offense?"

It's illegal for defensive players to shout out signals intending to confuse the offense's players — 5 yards for delay of game. Defenders may have their own signals to call, but they are not allowed to shout them out in a way to interfere with the offense's verbal signals. Better for a defense to stop a play with their bodies than their words.

Jerry Thompson

The center (55) is pointing to tell the offensive linemen what defensive player to count in figuring out their blocking assignments. The guards on each side of the center pass the information to the tackles next to them. The quarterback must stand back and wait for this flow of information or he may be running for his life when the ball is snapped.

18.

The
Blocking Game

When it comes to football, God is prejudiced towards big, fast kids.

— **Chuck Mills, coach, Utah State**

In the earliest days of college football, rules were rare. Players might resort to kicking or slugging to "block" an opponent. In 1886, the famous coach John Heisman observed: "The players stood upright and fought it out with each other hammer and tongs, tooth and nail, fist and feet. Fact is, you didn't stand much of a chance in those days unless you were a good wrestler and a fair boxer."

In the next two decades, the cumulative rule changes in blocking reduced the violent, unsportsmanlike behavior and injuries that critics cited in their resistance to the growing spectacle of football.

Blocking in football evolved to contact initiated by the blocker's shoulder against the tackler's body; the game became more orderly and less injurious. Techniques advanced further with blockers bringing their arms up in front of their chest horizontally, fist to fist, spreading their feet and bending their knees before contact. They could also leave their feet and lead with their shoulder in order to "teakettle" — upend — defenders who were running after the ball carrier. The only restrictions were that they couldn't block someone from behind — that was clipping — or hold them with their hands; that was holding. Coaches focused most of their teaching

Jerry Thompson

Both blockers have angles, positioned between their defender and the ball carrier, with excellent posture: heads up and feet balanced.

Jerry Thompson

How not to pass block: because the pad level of the offensive linemen (in white) is too high and the blockers are not square to the defender, their hands are not on the "blocking frame" of the rusher. Thus, he's able to breach their "cup" protection. The ultimate result, however? A 10-yard holding penalty.

on the blockers using their shoulders.

"What, specifically, do the rules say about blocking now?"

Offensive players are allowed to use their bodies and hands to block for the ball carrier, with certain restrictions. The rules state that "blocking is obstructing an opponent by contacting him with any part of the blocker's body; pushing is blocking an opponent with an open hand."

As a result, in today's game, using the shoulders has been mostly replaced by the use of the hands, resulting in more of a push; and holding is allowed under certain circumstances. The permitted area to hold is the "frame" of the defender's body — the area of the chest, from waist to neck, inside the arms.

A holding penalty may be whistled when the blocker holds outside the frame of the defender, though it's a difficult call for referees to make because of all the hand-fighting going on between seven blockers and defenders. Suffice it to say there's lots of rumbling and tumbling going on, like when the doors open on a Black Friday department-store sale.

Watch the big boys along the line of scrimmage as the ball is snapped; everything starts with the hands. You'll see seven sets of hands extend to contact the opponent, attempting to push and turn the defender away from the ball carrier while the hands of the defense extend to fight off the blocks. If you watch a defensive lineman against an offensive lineman, you'll see what amounts to a Ninja Turtle martial arts battle.

Because of this combat, arm and shoulder strength is critical for both offensive and defensive linemen; it's become a contest of bench pressing. Star football players are judged by their speed and skill in using their hands just as much as their running and reaction speed. This and weight training are critically important for football players, particularly linemen.

"What's leverage got to do with it?"

A few years ago, Stanford destroyed Oregon in the trenches by demonstrating, play after play, the most basic fundamental to the game of football: leverage. After struggling against Oregon State's undersized defensive line the game before, coach David Shaw observed that the Beavers were getting "under the pads" of the Cardinal offensive line and knocking them off the line of scrimmage. As a result, in practice, the Cardinal's big boys dedicated themselves to getting their shoulder pad levels down. Judging by their crushing victory the next Saturday against Oregon, their adjustment was successful.

Jerry Thompson

"Low man wins:" Defenders in white with lower pad levels have the advantage over the offensive linemen trying to block them. Note the defenders' posture: head and eyes up.

Leverage means that when you're blocking, tackling, or fighting off a blocker, "low man wins." It's simple physics: The lower player gets to use his legs and the higher player can only use his arms. Legs are stronger than arms.

This leverage can only be achieved if the player has contacted the opponent with the correct force and angle. If he engages an opponent while standing straight up, he will be flat footed, and have little force — nor can he get low enough in time before the contact. Usually being too high or lacking force originates with the player's stance and his first two steps out of that stance.

"How important is an offensive lineman's stance?"

Watch those offensive linemen who go from an "up" position — two-point stance, no hand on the ground. This lends itself to being too high when the player comes out of his stance at the snap of the ball. It's harder to get the shoulder level down before making contact with defenders. The advantage of the "up" position is that the linemen have a better view of all the defenders.

Watch to see how those linemen struggle in getting their shoulder level down while attempting to block. The correct stance allows the player to fire out low and hard with a flat back so that the force and angle can be quick and strong. When linemen become fatigued, they will start standing up, straightening their legs, and losing their leverage; watch for this in the fourth quarter of hard-fought games.

"Do offenses really hold on every play?"

In the past, there was a penalty for "illegal use of the hands," which was usually holding and restraining the defender. Today, referees could call holding on blockers — grabbing the player or his jersey — nearly every play because they are either cheating or because the defender moved in a surprise direction, and the offensive player found his hands outside the "blocking frame." Officials will generally call holding if the hold comes at the point of attack or is blatantly influential in the play's outcome.

"In blocking, what's a 'punch'"?

The "punch" is delivered by two fists in an explosive move to the chest by the blocker, so fast, hopefully, defenders can't react in time to defend their center of gravity. (Ask an offensive line coach for a demonstration and you won't be able to sleep on your stomach for a month). This is another reason the bench press is one of the most important weight exercises the offensive linemen do in the weight room.

"Can an offensive player block a defender below the waist?"

Injury prevention has become such an emphasis among officials that some blocking rules have been modified in the past 30 years. Formally, blocking below the waist at all times was legal and now it's limited. Today, there's no blocking below the waist on any kick or interception return because the defenders often can't see the offensive players who are coming to block them. Serious injuries come from open-field, below-the-waist blocks. It takes discipline for a blocker to resist the chance to make a big hit on a player who doesn't see him coming. Television, with its dramatic marketing of "big hits," is an obstacle to coaches who are trying to coach their players to check their egos and follow the rules. Football guidelines now protect those defenders who are considered in a "defenseless" position — and offensive players must buy into this or they and their team will pay the price.

Blockers moving from outside the formation towards the line of scrimmage may contact a defender above the waist and then slide down below the waist to finish the block. You will see these kinds of blocks in the secondary and sometimes on the outside defender on the line of scrimmage.

Unfortunately, if the referee misses the initial contact and just witnesses the low block, a penalty may be called on what's actually a legal block.

"What is a chop block?"

A "chop block" is when two blockers block a pass rusher at the same time, one blocking the defender's upper body, the other at the defender's knees. This can lead to serious injury. Teams will often double-team a key pass rusher, but unless both are blocking above the waist, the high blocker must disengage before the other blocker cuts the defender low.

"What's the difference between a "chop block" and a "cut block?"

A chop, as mentioned, is a high-low double block. A cut block is when a blocker contacts the defender below the waist, effectively knocking his legs out from under him.

"What is a combo block?"

A combo block occurs on a running play when the center has a defender on his nose. The guard next to him steps toward the center, taking over his man and enabling the center to step to the second level to block a linebacker. If the center has to block the nose by himself, the guard steps towards the center to protect that gap, and then goes to the second level. The combo block is also performed between tight ends and tackles and tackles and guards in the same way.

This interplay of blocking responsibilities and teamwork is a fascinating part of the game. It also happens in pass blocking when the center and guard trade blocking assignments on defenders who are criss-crossing on a stunt. (The combination pass blocking can also happen between a guard and a tackle.) If an offense can't effectively combo-block it is doomed and can count on watching everyone else in televised bowl games come season's end.

"What is a block in the back?"

A block in the back occurs when an offensive player, while having one or both feet on the ground, contacts a defender — and the force of the initial contact is from behind and above the waist. The penalty

The linemen pulling outside from their positions combo block, the tackle leaving a defender (on ground) to the blocker coming behind him so he can pursue a second-level block, probably on a linebacker.

for a block in the back is 10 yards from where the foul occurred. A similar block but below the waist is called clipping, and carries a 15-yard penalty from the spot.

Coaching Points

It's unfortunate that some coaches teach their players to hold and how to avoid being caught in the process. Many of the techniques involve a grab of the defender to stop momentum or direction, followed by a quick push that makes it hard to see the hold because of the separation of the move in the end. Most of the culprits are offensive linemen, many who are demonstrating skills better suited for pickpockets or magicians.

Defensive players have their own way of holding, mostly of pass receivers attempting to get free in the secondary. A defensive back tugging at the side of a receiver's jersey or hooking part of his body with an arm are common on pass plays, especially on "streak" routes. It is interference if a defender grabs the arm or hand of the receiver; in such cases, he's deemed to be playing the man and not the ball.

"Why are there so many penalties on kick returns?"

Coaches often get into arguments with referees about a block-in-the-back penalty, especially on kick returns, when a ball carrier reverses his direction, which changes his blocker's angle of contact. Because the blocker may not know where the runner is, he may initiate contact legally, but it becomes illegal because the would-be tackler turns at the last second in pursuit of the changed-direction runner.

"There's nothing that cleanses your soul like getting the hell kicked out of you."
— **Woody Hayes, coach Ohio State**

Sometimes a block-in-the-back penalty, called or uncalled, is not a penalty because "the position of the blocker's head or feet does not necessarily indicate the point of initial contact." (As an official, try talking that through with an angry coach who's in your face and badly needs breath mints.)

On punt returns, it's a challenge for coaches to teach blockers to be patient and conservative in their blocking decisions because that goes against the instinctual, all-out nature of the game. When a punt-return team player sees an opponent coming who doesn't see him, he wants to blast him with a big hit. But with officials looking for such cases, coaches now tell players to pull up and not hit the defender at all if he thinks it could be construed as a penalty.

You will occasionally see a player who can't, or doesn't care to, show restraint. After the penalty is called, watch him walk off the field and see what his reception is like from the coach. Some coaches will bench such a player to reinforce the "learning."

19.

The Tackling Game

It isn't necessary to see a good tackle. You can hear it.

— **Knute Rockne, coach, Notre Dame**

Teams that tackle well win football games. Tackling takes two things: courage and good technique. Defensive players learn to tackle as individuals and as a group, which is called "gang tackling." The first time a player faces a ball carrier running at him can be frightening; for that reason, coaches teach tackling at a slow, controlled pace to start. A player needs to be strong through the legs, hips and shoulders, and be able to keep his head up, eyes open and deliver a blow that will stop a ball carrier in his tracks.

In the Early Days

In 1877, all tackling had to be above the waist. As a result, Princeton showed up for a game with Harvard wearing tight-fitting laced canvas jackets over their game jerseys, making it difficult for the Harvards to tackle the Tigers. After a lengthy argument play continued; Harvard lost the argument but won the game. In the years beyond, other colleges started using the tight jackets that were invented by Princeton player L.P. Smock, from whom the term "smocks" is derived.

At one point early on, a ball carrier who had been tackled and pinned to

Jerry Thompson

Good tacklers "break down," get their feet under control, with angles on the runner (left), which will result in a gang tackle. Notice the pursuers: they will "explode their eyes" on contact.

the ground was required to shout "tackle down" to end the play — like having to say "uncle" in a wrestling match. In one game, according to *Football Thru the Years,* a player was face down in a mud puddle and no one heard him say anything. When the pile unraveled, it was discovered the ball carrier had nearly drowned, water in his lungs preventing him from saying "tackle down." This near-tragedy spurred the rule that a runner, once down, did not have to say anything. The referee, instead, would rule the play over. In 1888, tackling below the waist was made legal, but not below the knees. This triggered the development of mass momentum plays on offense that ultimately threatened the existence of football in America because of the rash of injuries and fatalities that resulted.

"Why do some teams miss so many tackles?"

Defenders who have missed tackles can look at the film and see that most of those misses came for two reasons: (a) they weren't on balance or in a leveraged position or (b) they didn't take the proper angle on a ball carrier. If defenders are face-up on the runner and don't get the angle, the ball carrier can beat them two ways: run to either side or run the defender over. If the defender has an angle, but is out of control or gets his feet crossed, he still will miss badly; it's vital to have your legs spread and your knees flexed.

Other missed tackles come because the defender is overextended and not close enough to the runner to contact him with his shoulder. This leaves him trying to tackle with his arms extended — and any good runner can break arm tackles. Certain players will also miss a tackle because it's easier to be lazy with the fundamentals or the tackler does not have the aggressive drive — courage — necessary to make a tackle.

"How do you coach a player to be a good tackler?"

Smart defenders don't try for the "big hit" on a good runner in the open field — those mostly come on ball carriers who have one leg planted in the ground, or those whose head is down; woe unto them. When you have to tackle someone who has strong legs, NFL veteran Kam Chancellor advises, "hit the big guy anywhere, just get him down. There's no secret. It's all will, individual will. It's about getting there, wrapping up and bringing him down … understand you're going to take a big hit and hope the cavalry gets there."

"Exploding your hips" is the key to good tackling; thus do coaches spend much time on drills that promote this basic skill. It's like the swift move of a karate expert breaking a brick with his bare hands. The explosive power comes from intense focus and a compact blow delivered at great speed, generating the oomph to accomplish what might have seemed to be physically impossible.

You have to have balance and take an angle, hit with your shoulder and not your head, although you have to keep your head up and eyes open. Some tacklers miss as they anticipate the immediate hit and they unconsciously shut their eyes. Coaches tell their players, "Explode — forcefully *open* — your eyes when you tackle." See if you can see some players who might be shutting their eyes prematurely: they're the ones overextended and empty handed, with their heads down.

Gridiron Tradition

In the early game of football, players did not wear helmets; it wasn't until 1939 that they became mandatory. Although most of the contact was with the shoulder on both offense and defense, there was still the possibility of the heads, noses and faces getting bashed, not only from attempted tackles but kicks and punches as well. Broken noses were one of the most common injuries for players back then. One preventative measure taken

Jerry Thompson

Perfect form tackling: feet under control, legs underneath, not over extended, head up, exploding the hips, wrapping the arms and driving the ball carrier backwards.

was to let players grow out their hair in hopes that the shaggy coiffure would offer some protection. As players became bigger, stronger and faster, hairstyles gave way to leather helmets that could fold and cover the head when fastened with a chinstrap.

The evolution continued in the '50s with the development of hard-plastic suspension helmets that players, unfortunately, soon realized could deal a punishing blow when rammed into an opponent.

Soon after, colleges found they could imbed colors and symbols in the helmets and they became a signature brand of each team.

Coaching Points

Coaches have had to radically change the way they teach tackling because of concussions and other injuries that occurred when defenders began leading with their heads to tackle. Today, penalties are called on players who use their head as a weapon in hitting a player, resulting in a 15-yard penalty and, if severe enough, the guilty player being kicked out of the game — and, if the incident happens in the second half, suspended for half the following game as well.

"What's the difference between 'targeting' and 'unnecessary roughness?'"

The NCAA has outlined four major targeting criteria: (a) launching toward an opponent, contacting the head or neck area; (b) a crouch followed by a thrust with contact at the head or neck area; (c) leading with the helmet, forearm, fist, hand or elbow into the head or neck area; and (d) lowering the head, attacking and initiating with the crown of the helmet. The rules state that "no player shall target and initiate contact against the head or neck area of a defenseless opponent … if there's doubt, it's a foul."

Jerry Thompson

Sometimes a tackler has to simply grab hold and hope for help.

Unnecessary roughness is called for hitting after the whistle, blind-side blocking of a defender who is (a) nowhere near the runner; (b) out of bounds; or (c) using methods beyond what is necessary to block or tackle another player.

"Don't helmets protect the brain from concussion?"

The suspension and design of helmets spreads the blow, but are of no use in protecting the brain, which is free floating in fluid inside the skull. A blow to the head always concusses the brain inside the skull because there is nothing in it that can soften or cushion the contact. The changes to football rules regarding the use of the helmet in blocking and tackling should help reduce concussions, but the biggest improvement will come from coaches who teach the fundamentals of the game — and from the players, who must become more protective of their heads. This is the same concept the original players of the game had to learn because no one wore helmets.

Coaches and defensive players have worked feverishly on isometric neck exercises to strengthen their necks to help sustain the contact the head may receive. Neck and spinal injuries can result from a player tackling or blocking with his head and neck bowed down when contacting an opponent. The absolute principle in teaching safe tackling is: keep your head and eyes up, not only to see and be able to react to danger, but to keep the neck in the strongest, most supportive position.

"What's rugby got to do with tackling and blocking in football?"

As mentioned, because of injuries and litigation, coaches at all levels have come under pressure to discourage and ban tackling with the head as a prime point of contact. Those who play rugby learn not to use their head in contacting an opponent; they don't wear helmets. Instead, they all use their shoulders. Now, football players are being taught to keep their heads up, contact the ball carrier with their shoulder, wrap their arms and roll him to the ground, just as rugby players have been doing for more than 100 years. These skills have become important, and necessary, for the safety of the players and the survival of football.

20.

The Head Game

Football doesn't build character, it eliminates the weak ones.

— **Darryl Royal, coach, University of Texas**

In a book called *Football,* issued for the U.S. Naval Institute in 1943, the authors talked about building "esprit de corps: a football team must be strong in sacrificial quality, in courage and in loyalty or it will be impoverished in morale. Morale ... is the state of mind of the player founded upon knowledge of proper technique, attitude on and off the field, willingness to be expendable, pride in self and team, and enthusiasm for the game — all of these qualities having their culmination in well-based confidence.

"Well-based confidence gives a team its extra dash, its assurance, its poise; gives it the ability to outscore a rival of equal courage, equal fighting capacity, equal ability to win ... All the confidence in the world will not hurt a player if he resists the temptation to believe the next opponent can be easily beaten. But should the player coast mentally, even though he is putting in the practice hours faithfully, it will require considerable shock to bring him back to normal self-confidence."

"Coasting mentally" is when the players lose the focus necessary to overcome the mental challenges that occur during a football game: weather, injuries, bad penalty calls, dropped passes, offside penalties in the red zone (inside the 20 yard-line), blocked kicks, kicks run back for scores, interceptions, fumbles and failures on crucial third- and fourth-down conversions. The "considerable shock" would likely be a stunning defeat involving players who lack focus, commit mental errors and play with little intensity. The challenges that come in a football game can always be handled in a positive or negative way. How has your team handled adversity with the game on the line?

"If lessons are learned in defeat, our team is getting a great education."
— **Murray Warmath, coach, Minnesota**

If your team gives an underdog opponent the idea that it can play with the favored team, an upset becomes more possible. A favored team needs to establish itself both physically and mentally in the first half so the underdog loses any hope of winning.

The "head game" often decides the winners and losers in rival games, which are special because, every year, they often match players from the same state, sometimes even from the same high school. No game gets in a player's head like that of his hated rival, and the results can become heated and highly unpredictable, bringing a rich flavor of suspense to traditional rumbles. In 1982, I was a coach at Washington State (2-8) and we played the Washington Huskies (9-1) and were 34-point underdogs. The Cougars turned the football world upside down, winning 24-20 and knocking the Huskies out of the Rose Bowl. The longer the game went, the better WSU played and the worse the Huskies played. The Cougars had nothing to lose and the Huskies had everything to lose, which became a heavier burden for Washington as the game moved to its finale. You could feel it.

Losing Your Mojo

Losing your mojo "refers to a loss of inspiration, a loss of that special spark," says Craig Sigl, a mental toughness trainer. Like a failing patient, a football team's decline is marked by decreased mental toughness, which is the ability of an athlete and team to play at his highest level, and to not give up, regardless of the competitive circumstances. A team that is struggling will appear indecisive, undisciplined and lackadaisical. Often, coaches will resort to all sorts of tricks and psychology in an effort to regain the team's mojo: highlight films, loud music, guest speakers and other desperate measures to inspire enthusiasm. In the end, if the players don't make it happen on the field, play after play, there won't be any mojo at all.

How Do You Know?

When it vanishes, it can do so quickly — and without warning. What are the red flags for lost mojo? A team doesn't play lively or fast. The game drains, instead of energizing, players. A sense of weariness sets in. Finally, when opportunities arise, the team does not, or cannot, react with energy and confidence.

By the way, this applies to fans, too. They come to their feet more slowly, if at all, and just don't feel like belting out the school song when their team scores a meaningless touchdown while being trounced.

In preparation for games, some teams will increase their contact drills in an effort to regain their lost mojo. The hitting in football can be a psychological boost, especially if you're the player giving out the hit. Unfortunately, it can give players and coaches a false sense of how prepared and focused they are for a game; there's more to the game than hitting.

Watch the game outside the sidelines because it has a great deal to do with how the game is going inside the lines. Look to see which team seems excited and into the game. One team may be pumped and jumping while the other team loses its enthusiasm and looks "ho hum."

Are the players getting in and out of the huddle quickly or trotting like "dead men walking?" The walkers are usually getting worn down on the field and on the scoreboard.

Check for penalties, particularly procedure or after-the-whistle fouls; both indicate a lack of focus and discipline. When there's a turnover, check how the team that forced the turnover reacts: does it capitalize and score points or does it squander the opportunity? Both outcomes have a huge psychological impact for, and against, a team.

Delice Coffey, a football psychologist, said, "When an athlete focuses on a past mistake, their mindset becomes negative, and this destroys mental toughness."

How can you see mental toughness being destroyed? Watch for turnovers or careless penalties.

Look at the players' body language on the sideline. Are their heads down, not in the game? Do the coaches emit confidence, or do they appear angry, lax or out of control? Does it look like the players are being positive with each other?

Jerry Thompson

A happy defensive unit celebrates a recovered fumble. A turnover can be a big psychological boost for the offense and excite the crowd as well as deflating the opponent.

"How do teams prepare themselves psychologically?"

Chip Kelly, former head coach at Oregon, was a master psychologist, preparing his team the same way for every "faceless" opponent. He preached the mantra that his team needed, everyday, to "water the bamboo," a phrase that he picked up from an inspirational speaker, Greg Bell. The phrase referred to the idea that when you plant bamboo, you water it for two years before it shows any growth at all. Still, you have to have faith, to keep tending the bamboo religiously, despite seeing minimal growth. Ultimately, however, it shoots up strong and grows fast.

An Old-fashioned Pep Talk

In the early days of college football, it was said that Notre Dame Coach Knute Rockne, anxious to "fire up" his players for a rival game, told the story of a former player on his deathbed imploring the coach to "tell the boys, when they're up against it, win one for the Gipper" before running out on the field. Years ago, the head coach of Texas A&M had a longhorn steer castrated in front of his team the day before their Thanksgiving rival game with the Texas Longhorns, much to the displeasure of everyone except his football team. These are extreme cases of using tricks and demonstrations to psychologically motivate football teams for important games. Obviously, the cruel use of animals in attempting to rouse the team has been curtailed as mores and common decency have evolved. Today, bonfires and pep rallies still are eagerly anticipated and attended by students and alumni at such schools as Notre Dame and UCLA.

Regardless of how they do it, successful coaches have the ability to energize players. But it's a balancing act. As the big game approaches, players can get carried away by the hype and lose the focus needed to play at a high level. Thus, assignments, techniques and training must remain the priority in game preparation.

"Should players worry about losing?"

Worrying about losing can be the kiss of death for football teams. Kelly's notion of focusing on preparation greatly increases the chances of a favorable outcome. With this approach, every game becomes the same, whether conference, non-conference or involving a rival.

Every opponent is prepared for the same way. This helps prevent the uneven performances that may cripple a team: the highs and lows of a team that "peaks" for its rival and then the following week is lethargic playing its next, very beatable, opponent.

"Emotion is highly overrated in football. My wife Corky is emotional as hell but can't play football worth a damn."
— **John McKay, coach USC**

If an athlete concentrates on the outcome of the game rather than doing his best on each play, nervousness will work against him. Because he may be afraid to lose, he will make more mistakes and not perform to his best level. So, the best chance for success is to focus entirely on each play as it happens.

For a team, success is not always winning, by the way, because sometimes a brave effort expended in a losing outcome is a "moral victory." Although coaches are loath to admit it, gutsy, all-out efforts can represent a victory for a team that's trying to be more competitive. Coaches tell their players to "lay it all on the field, hold nothing back." Not many coaches would — or should — be disappointed with a team that does that, win or lose.

"Doesn't what happened in past games affect the next game?"

Another mental shift that can occur before a big game is for players to dwell on what happened in the past. As they say, you can ruin a perfectly good future by worrying about it. A player can't change the past, an effective coach assures him, but he can learn from it so he doesn't repeat mistakes. As counselors urge their clients: "If something bad happened in the past, learn and let it go." A team and its athletes can't control the future, but they can control their present and how they think and react to the adversity that naturally comes up in the presence of high-level competition.

"How do players keep a positive attitude when there's so much at stake?"

This is where great coaches who know how to connect and communicate with their players make a decisive difference. Players may find themselves with negative thoughts before a big game. Great coaches help players avoid that by getting them to visualize themselves doing their assignments properly, which instills confidence. It also helps for the coach to visualize — and treat his players — as if they're already doing the right things, which promotes confidence in everybody. Having a positive attitude doesn't make up for a lack of talent or preparation, but it does give the athletes the best possible chance of playing to their competitive potential. And helps players develop mental toughness.

If players worry about their opponent or teammates, they won't play to their best ability because doing so fuzzies their focus. Players should, instead, concentrate on improving their own performance. This is much more difficult to accomplish on the field against a motivated opponent than talking about it in the locker room.

21.

Rules of the Game

There are several differences between a football game and a revolution. For one thing, a football game usually lasts longer and the participants wear uniforms

— Alfred Hitchcock, film director

It's late in a game and the home team has just scored a 75-yard touchdown to take the lead. Players bump chests. Coaches throw their fists in the air. Fans go wild. But, wait, what's this?

"This" is another element to the game that's a huge, but often overlooked, factor in who wins. This is a penalty. No touchdown.

"Block in the back on No. 57," says the ref into his microphone. "The result is no touchdown. First and 10 at the 25 yard-line." Sticking to the rules of the game is critical for football teams, some of whom learn the lesson the hard way. So, what are the rules of the game?

"What's the difference between a touchback and a safety?"

Nearly everybody mixes these two up, so knowing the difference puts you in elite status. A touchback is when the ball becomes dead in the possession of a player behind his own goal line, or a kick or fumble becomes

OFFICIAL FOOTBALL SIGNALS
HIGH SCHOOL AND COLLEGE

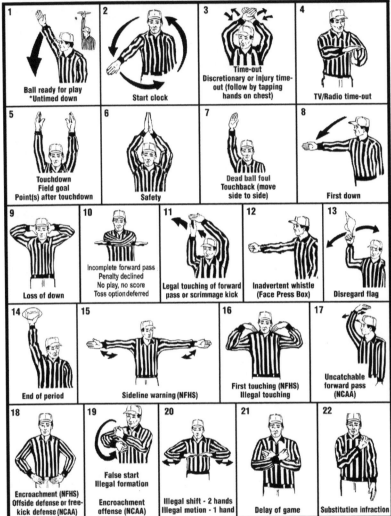

1 — Ball ready for play *Untimed down	2 — Start clock	3 — Time-out Discretionary or injury time-out (follow by tapping hands on chest)	4 — TV/Radio time-out
5 — Touchdown Field goal Point(s) after touchdown	6 — Safety	7 — Dead ball foul Touchback (move side to side)	8 — First down
9 — Loss of down	10 — Incomplete forward pass Penalty declined No play, no score Toss option deferred	11 — Legal touching of forward pass or scrimmage kick	12 — Inadvertent whistle (Face Press Box)	13 — Disregard flag
14 — End of period	15 — Sideline warning (NFHS)	16 — First touching (NFHS) Illegal touching	17 — Uncatchable forward pass (NCAA)
18 — Encroachment (NFHS) Offside defense or free-kick defense (NCAA)	19 — False start Illegal formation Encroachment offense (NCAA)	20 — Illegal shift - 2 hands Illegal motion - 1 hand	21 — Delay of game	22 — Substitution infraction

OFFICIAL FOOTBALL SIGNALS
HIGH SCHOOL AND COLLEGE

23 Failure to wear required equipment	24 Illegal helmet contact	25 Illegal Horse-Collar Tackle	27 Unsportsmanlike conduct Noncontact foul	28 Illegal participation
29 Sideline interference (Face Press Box)	30 Running into or Roughing kicker or holder	31 Illegal batting/kicking (Followed by pointing toward toe for kicking)	32 Invalid fair catch signal (NFHS) Illegal fair catch signal	33 Forward pass interference Kick catching interference
34 Roughing passer	35 Illegal pass/forward handing (Face Press Box)	36 Intentional grounding	37 Ineligible downfield on pass	38 Personal foul
39 Clipping	40 Blocking below waist Illegal block	41 Chop block	42 Holding/obstructing Illegal use of hands/arms	43 Illegal block in the back
44 Helping runner Interlocked blocking	45 Grasping face mask or helmet opening	46 Tripping	47 Disqualification	

dead behind the defending team's goal line and the other team is responsible for the ball ending up there. In such situations, the ball will be brought out to the 20-yard line with possession awarded to the defending team.

It's a safety if the ball becomes dead in the possession of a player behind his own goal line and his own team is responsible for the ball being there. This happens when a quarterback is sacked in his own end zone, or a running back starting a few yards deep in his own end zone is tackled before he can get out. Getting caught in your own end zone costs your team two points; same story if your punter's blocked punt goes "through" the end zone. In both cases, the team giving up the score is required to kick the ball to its opponent from its 20-yard line.

Final word: When in doubt, it's a touchback and not a safety.

"If a player intercepts a pass on his own 3-yard line and is tackled in his own end zone, is it a safety for the other team?"

It's not a safety if the player's original momentum carries him into his own end zone; the player has up to his own 5-yard line to measure that momentum. If his momentum takes him into the end zone, and if the ball is declared dead in his possession in the end zone, the ball belongs to the player's team at the spot where he gained possession. If he deliberately runs into the end zone, and — not by his own momentum — is tackled, then, yes, it's a safety.

"What plays can be reviewed by instant replay?"

Reviewable scoring plays include a potential touchdown or safety, or a field goal attempt, only if the ball was above the crossbar and lower than the top of the uprights. If the ball is higher than the top of the uprights, it may not be reviewed.

Pass plays that may be reviewed are those that are complete, incomplete or intercepted anywhere on the field of play or end zone. Reviews may also be made to determine if a pass was touched by an ineligible or eligible player or an official — or whether a ball was handed or passed forwards or backwards.

Reviews may also be made to determine potential dead balls and loose balls ruled fumbles, incomplete or completed passes and ball carriers' forward progress.

Kick plays that may be reviewed include touching of a kick, a scrimmage kick crossing the neutral zone and kicking-team players blocking before they are eligible to touch the ball on an onside kickoff. Officials can also review the number of players on the field for either team during a live ball and make clock adjustments when rulings are reversed.

"How is a video review conducted?"

Different conferences may have different rules but they must be the same for all the teams in the same conference. In the Pac-12, a crew of officials reviews every play on video that is continuously streaming in the press box. If the press box crew observes a play that should be reviewed, they can buzz the referee on the field to notify him they are going to take a second look.

A review can be avoided, and not slow the game down, if the press box crew determines there is no need for one.

In other cases, the referee on the field can request a review or either coach can have a play reviewed, but only if the play in question qualifies as reviewable. Non-reviewable plays, for example, would be most penalty calls or lack thereof, or a play that is whistled dead by the officials before the play could come to its rightful end.

Coaches have a limit of two requests per game, although if the first is overruled that coach doesn't get the second request and his team is charged with a timeout. If the review is reversed, the coach will get a second request for the rest of the game and his team is not charged a time out. Most coaches will save their request for the latter, more critical stages of the game.

"What are the conditions to conduct an instant replay review?"

There has to be reasonable evidence that an error was made in an on-field ruling, the actual play is reviewable, and the review would have a direct impact on the game. It's just coincidental to frustrated and impatient coaches that when making a review, the referee has to slowly jog half the field to confer with the press box crew, then back again. Experienced fans can often squeeze in a quick bathroom break during the lull of a review.

"How many officials are involved on the field and what are their responsibilities?"

There are eight officials, with the referee — the leader of the crew — having the final say in decisions. He's also the one communicating the signals to the crowd, always, of course, facing the television cameras.

The rest of the crew consists of the:

♦ Umpire: primarily responsible for spotting the ball at the beginning of each play;

♦ Head linesman: responsible for the chains used to verify how many yards a team has covered during a play, also for counting how many downs a team has used and how many it has left;

♦ Line judge: responsible for time keeping and helping the linesman set up the line of scrimmage;

♦ Back judge: responsible for monitoring the duration of timeouts and halftime;

♦ Field judge: stands toward the rear of the field and makes sure players are in-bounds and supervises defensive players who are often placed "deep," a distance away from the rest of the players, and, thus, would make some of the pass interference judgments;

♦ Side judges (two): responsible for determining whether players remain in-bounds and supervising play on their side of the field.

"What is pass interference?"

You can figure out pass interference for yourself, but you'll need to remember the following before you do: physical contact is required to establish interference and each player has territorial rights to go for the ball. "Incidental contact" is not pass interference if each player is making a "bona fide" effort to reach the pass.

This is where all the arguments start: what constitutes "incidental contact" and "bona fide?" The rules explain that if the intent of the player is obvious: making an attempt to impede by tackling or grasping a receiver or any other intentional contact before he touches the pass is evidence that the defender is playing the man and disregarding the ball and his actions are therefore illegal.

A player who tackles or runs into a receiver when a forward pass is obviously underthrown or overthrown is disregarding the ball and his actions are illegal. However, this is not pass interference but unnecessary roughness or targeting.

Flagrant offenders are disqualified — and if the penalty occurs in the second half of a game, the guilty party must not only miss the rest of the game, but half of the team's next game, too. This penalty is in response to concerns for safety of players who don't see the defender and are in a "defenseless position."

Jerry Thompson

If the ball came loose right after this picture was shot, it would be a "reviewable play": fumble or not? If the ball comes loose after the player is officially down, no, because the ground can't cause a fumble.

Pass interference rules do not apply after a player or an official has touched the pass anywhere inbounds; for example, if a pass is tipped by a defender at the line of scrimmage, a defensive back would be free to contact a receiver trying to catch that pass.

The penalty for pass interference on the defense in the NFL is an automatic first down at the point of the foul, while in college rules, it is an automatic first down at the spot of the foul or 15 yards if the foul occurred more than 15 yards down field.

College coaches may gladly accept a 15-yard pass interference penalty against their team if the deliberate foul prevents a 50-yard touchdown. Pass interference isn't just a defensive players' penalty, it can be called on offensive receivers as well. The penalty for offensive interference is 10 yards and loss of down.

"What is the difference between running into the kicker and roughing the kicker?"

The penalty for roughing is 15 yards while running into the kicker is only 5 yards. The difference in the fouls is that roughing is a live-ball personal foul that endangers the kicker or holder. Running into the kicker or holder is "displacing them from their kicking or holding position," but they are not considered to have been "roughed."

Incidental contact is not a foul and the kicker's protection ends when he's had a reasonable amount of time to regain his balance. If a defensive player is blocked into the kicker or holder, and if a rushing player touches the kick before contacting the holder or kicker: no foul.

Referees have been known to miss instances of defenders being pushed into the place kicker or punter, perhaps owing to the relatively weak political power that kickers possess. (For starters, they might weigh 160 pounds, be on the field for only a handful of plays and wear helmets that include those wimpy single-bar facemasks.)

A coach whose team has forced the opponent into a punting situation should consider the consequences of a penalty before deciding to block the kick. If the opponent has fewer than five yards to go for a first down, don't do it. If a player runs into the kicker, the penalty will give the opponent a first down. The same goes if you have the opponent pinned back, fourth and fewer than 15 yards to go for a first down. Rough the kicker, even accidentally, and it will be an automatic first down that will inflate the other team and take the wind out of the offending team's sails.

Keep in mind that many punters are also drama majors, and like a World Cup soccer player, can swoon in what looks like a horrendous collision, but without the collision part. A particularly dramatic swoon may draw an immediate crescendo of "boos" from the home crowd and can help referees fall for this charade, so coaches need to really think through decisions to block punts.

Statistics

"What are the most important statistics for defense?"

Rushing defense has always been at the top of the list. If your team has a defense that controls the opponent's running game and forces the offense to pass the ball, your team has a huge advantage.

Turnover margin is another significant statistical category. The number of fumbles and interceptions made by a team's offense is important, but the number of takeaways by the defense can be even more de-cisive; all good teams take the ball away from their opponents more often than their opponents take the ball away from them.

Finally, it's hard to argue with "average-points-allowed-per-game" as the most important statistic because if you score more points than you give up, you obviously have a winning team.

Traditionally, offense gets more attention than defense because scoring points is fun to watch and keeping the opponent from scoring not so much. This is indicative of most sports and games: offense is glamorous while defense is tedious and hard work. The runners, passers, receivers and even kickers get more attention and publicity than good defensive players, yet it's the defense that makes the difference in any evenly matched contest.

Universities will often choose an offensive coordinator over a defensive coach when selecting a new head coach. The hire offers the potential of a new, exciting offense that might score lots of points and trigger lots of ticket sales. Currently, offense and high-scoring games are the rage and low-scoring defensive struggles rare. But if you're going to be an educated football fan, watch how the defensive players play the game. Occasionally, they will score points on their own, but their skills and athleticism go large-ly unnoticed by the unsophisticated spectator.

"What are the most important statistics for offense?"

Offensive skill players have an advantage because there are more stats kept for offense than defense — and, based on this, some might say offen-sive football is more fun than defense, both to play and to watch.

Quarterbacks are judged by their passing efficiency: figured by ratios based on average yards gained per pass attempts and completions, total yards gained, touchdowns and interceptions. Running backs are judged by average yards per pass reception, yards per rush, touchdowns per attempt and fumbles per attempt. Recently another category has been added — av-erage yards gained after contact by a tackler. Receivers are rated by aver-age receptions per game, yards per game, touchdowns per game, yards per catch and yards gained after the catch.

The poor offensive linemen get most of their attention when their jer-sey number is called out over the stadium's loudspeaker whenever they are called for a penalty. Offensive line coaches have developed rating systems that judge the big guys on their rates of performing the proper assignment and technique for every play of the game. They get extra credit for "pan-cakes" — flattening an opponent with a crushing block. Such video clips, in post-game film sessions, are run back and forth to the delight of the team.

Both offensive and defensive teams are rated by total yards, points per game and separate categories for running and passing.

A Formula for Predicting Victory

Based on extensive studies of college football game outcomes, **footballstudyhall.com** describes five factors that have the most influence on who wins on the gridiron: explosiveness, efficiency, field position, finishing drives and turnovers.

Explosiveness is measured by yards per-play and efficiency is measured by third-down conversion rates. Field position is rated by average field position when starting an offensive drive. Finishing drives is measured by red-zone scoring and a newer rubric that is more accurate: points per-trip inside the opponents' 40-yard line. Turnovers have always been critical turning points in football games and the best teams have margins that are positive, i.e., they away the ball more than they give it up.

> *"Nobody in football should be called a genius. A genius is a guy like Norman Einstein."*
>
> **— Joe Theisman, NFL quarterback**

Based on studies, **footballstudyhall.com** has determined your chances of winning the game if you win a particular statistical category: winning the explosiveness battle, 86% of the time you win; the efficiency battle, 83% of the time; points-per-trip inside the 40-yard line battle, 75% of the time; the field position battle (using average starting position per drive), 72% of the time; and the turnover battle, 73% of the time.

Now that you know all this, keep track of these statistics while you're watching your favorite team and see if the odds prove true.

22.

Gamebreakers for Players

Coaching is nothing more than eliminating mistakes before you get fired.

— **Lou Holtz, coach, Notre Dame**

Nobody is perfect. You've probably mentally thrown a few penalty flags regarding information I've shared. As an author, maybe I've stepped on the literary out-of-bounds line here or offered an unsportsmanlike metaphor there. And players blow it, too. You can learn to recognize those blunders that are pivotal in deciding who wins and loses. Here's my list of gamebreakers for players:

1. A wide receiver should never be offside. They should always be looking in at the ball and not move until they see the center move the ball on the snap. There is no reason whatsoever to be offside, particularly on running plays when everyone knows you don't want to hit anybody, anyway.

2. A player covering a kick should never follow the same-color jersey running down the field. This opens up holes in the coverage as the players get too bunched together. The player following should move one way or another to fill the empty lane, width-wise.

3. Players covering kicks should "break down" at least two to three yards in front of the kick returner in order to be under control to make

the tackle. Those who don't are easily faked out by the return man, overrun him or are pushed out of the way by a blocker they can't see coming. For a player, it's a sickening feeling to watch a returner running scot-free in the lane you were supposed to be in.

4. On a play where the ball carrier has broken well ahead of his blockers, those blocking should resist the temptation to make a needless block on a player who has little chance of catching the runner. It risks a costly penalty that will negate the runner's gain. Such a player will be punished in three ways: by a penalty from the referee, a tongue-lashing from his coach and a snub by his ex-best friend who just had his 95-yard touchdown run nullified by the guy's bonehead mistake.

> *"Treat a player as he is, and he will remain as he is. Treat him as what he could be and he will become what he should be."*
>
> — Jimmy Johnson, coach, Dallas Cowboys

5. While attempting to tackle, players should not leave their feet and overextend their bodies and arms. They should keep their legs underneath them for balance, control and power. It looks weak and their coach and teammates will think they're afraid when they leave their feet behind — in an impossible position — to make a tackle.

6. Players should never touch an official except to thank him and shake his hand after the game.

7. Players should never play "police officer" and try to pull other players off a pile up. It can cause a brawl and it's a penalty if they do. They should restrict their community service to the homeless shelter on weekends.

8. If a defender is playing deep pass defense, he should never let a receiver get behind him — unless he doesn't value his own life. The reception he gets from teammates on the sidelines may be colder than a playoff game in Green Bay.

9. If a team blocks a punt and it goes beyond the line of scrimmage, a player shouldn't try and pick it up and run with it. The opponent can't advance it where it is and if he tries to pick it up and fumbles it, the other team can advance it. Either team can advance a

Jerry Thompson

Jerry Thompson

The difference between making a tackle (top) and missing one (bottom) is that the defender has his legs and feet under him, while the other's are overextended, allowing the runner to push him away.

blocked kick if it's behind the line of scrimmage.

10. A player should never give up the ball to another player while submerged in a pile of players. Sometimes, it will end up in the hands of a persuasive member of the other team.

11. A player should never retaliate if an opposing player punches or kicks him. The referee usually misses the instigator and catches the retaliator. It can be a 15-yard penalty or disqualification and ejection from the game, a grim reward for attempting to establish justice.

12. A player should never duck his head when making a block or tackle as it puts his neck and spine in an extremely vulnerable position. That's asking for a broken neck. A player's head and eyes should always be up when making contact with an opponent.

13. A quarterback should always hold the ball with two hands close to his body, until he throws it or tucks it away to run with it. Often, a quarterback has the ball ripped away from him by a pass rusher he doesn't see while he's looking for his own pass receivers.

14. A defender who is responsible for "setting the edge" — containing — should never allow a ball carrier to get around him outside, towards the sideline. If that happens every other defender must adjust their position to cover for his mistake. He should prepare to be blistered in the team's film session.

15. A player should never commit a foul after the whistle has been blown to end a play. Those who do are merely submitting to their own ego, and don't have the best interests of the team in mind. It's definitely not cool for his family and girl friend to watch him get chewed out by the coach and sent to languish on the bench. So much for glory.

16. All defenders should hit blockers with their inside shoulder and keep their outside arm free. If they don't, they lose leverage and give up big gains on inside and outside plays.

23.

Gamebreakers for Coaches

On this team, we're all united in a common goal: to keep my job.

— Lou Holtz, coach, Notre Dame

Sometimes, fans can be too tough on coaches. It's easy making a play call from Row 62; not as easy when you're the coach and know that the star player dogged it in practice all week and fumbled three times in Thursday's drills.

Be that as it may, coaches do make mistakes and if they make too many they might awake on Sunday morning to find a For Sale sign in their front yard. Here are crucial gamebreakers for coaches:

1. Don't waste timeouts. Save them to control the clock late in the first or second half, or use them when their team is absolutely exhausted.

2. Never waste a timeout to avoid a delay of game penalty on a kick for point-after-touchdown or short field goal. A 5-yard penalty should not impact the kicker on a short kick; so a coach should take it.

3. Never waste a timeout trying to figure out what to do on a short-yardage or fourth-down situation. That should have been figured out in the coaches' staff meeting and practiced by Thursday before the game. Having a play already selected can cause the defense to hurry its own decision making, which could lead to a mistake the offense can exploit.

4. When setting up for a game-winning field goal, never call a play

with the potential to get the ball out of the position the kicker prefers, meaning usually the center of the field. The closer to the goal line, the worse (sharper) the angle for a place kick from the hash mark; get it in the middle for best results.

5. Never go for touchdowns on fourth-and-goal against a tough, conservative opponent early in the game when a "chip shot" field goal is easily makeable and may prove extremely significant in a close game. The fans will boo, but they're not looking ahead to what may be a low-scoring game in which every point counts. Not scoring at all is a deflating blow to the offense and a big psychological boost to the defense. And if the team is on the road, feeds the frenzy of the crowd, which can be a very scary sound.

> *"We can't run. We can't pass. We can't stop the run. We can't stop the pass. We can't kick. Other than that, we're just not a very good football team right now."*
>
> — Bruce Coslet, coach, New York Jets

6. If winning the coin toss, don't elect to kick off into the wind. If a team wants to kick off, they should choose the prevailing wind because the other team will not use its choice to kick into that wind, unless the coaches and captains miscommunicate or just plain make a foolish choice.

7. Don't assume a captain knows the choices his coach wants on the coin flip. Coaches should practice the coin toss with their captains before the players go out on the field. Although it looks like a friendly circle of friends out there at the 50-yard line, the players are pumped up and intense, the perfect state to make a mistake.

8. Avoid letting "hunches" get in the way of disciplined, well-researched defensive play-calling. Hunches are fine, but defensive coaches align their players not knowing what play may be called; they may have a prediction based on scouting films of games, but they never know for sure. At all times, coaches have to make their players aware of what they must be prepared to defend, no matter what the circumstances.

9. Don't call for a punt block when an opponent has fourth and

less than five yards to go for a first down. As mentioned, if a player attempting to block the kick runs into the kicker, even by accident, a 5-yard penalty will give the opponent a first down.

10. **If a team's offense is clicking, don't attempt to block a punt when the opponent has less than 15 yards to go for a first down.** Roughing the kicker is a 15-yard penalty that will give the opponent a first down, a psychological rush, and prevent your offense from coming on the field with some momentum. This can be an overwhelming psychological boost to a team on its first possession of a half.

11. **Always have the "hands" team on the field if an onside kick is likely.** A coach needs to have his best ball handlers within the 10-yard neutral zone. That situation could be toward the end of the game or when the team kicking — because of a penalty on the other team on the previous play — is doing so from near midfield: an opportunity to gain possession by an onside kick with a reduced risk of losing precious field position.

12. **Never be assessed a penalty for offside or illegal procedure. It's a sign of poor teamwork, concentration, and/or coaching.** All players should be watching the ball and restrict their charge until it moves with the center snap. Obviously, tension, fatigue and crowd noise can disrupt the focus of players on either side, but coaches must prepare their players to meet this challenge in daily practices, before the game begins.

13. **Beware of his team's tendencies — going into the game and during the game.** A coach should always keep track of them; his opponent certainly is. Many coaches overlook a successful play because they don't call it enough. Other coaches stubbornly call plays that aren't working or don't vary their snap count, which gives the defense the opportunity of getting an extra step on penetrating the offensive formation.

14. **Don't get desperate until it's time to get desperate. Many a coach has called a fake punt or an all-out blitz before the ideal time.** For example, early in a game, running a fake punt from midfield against the defense's "safe punt" alignment is unwise. Good coaches know when to "fold 'em" and when to go for it. A basic mistake is to try something tricky too early in the game when the opponent might be more alert and cautious. Better to try the tricks when the opponent is off balance and losing focus — and not suspecting a fake in the least. It also helps to have an opponent thoroughly scouted so coaches and players know their opponent's tendencies well enough to capitalize on their predictability.

15. **In a last-minute offensive drive, concern yourself more with not "wasting time" than with "saving time."** Sometimes, waiting until the end of the game (to use timeouts) wastes time, leaving you with little time on

the clock.

16. A coach should never criticize a player until he has asked himself if he fully prepared that player in a practice situation to perform the assignment or technique he expected in the game. Too often, coaches lambast a player before they evaluate their own diligence and performance in preparing that player. A coach can *expect* what he *accepts* on the practice field.

17 Don't be in a negative emotional state when reviewing game films with the team and especially so, not with a hangover. It's helpful to have the review session more than a day after the game so everyone can calm down and evaluate what needs to improve and what was done well.

Coaches who tongue-lash players for poor performance in front of the whole team usually regret it the next day when they watch the films again with clearer heads and better perspective. It can be disastrous for the morale of the team and can lead to the coach "losing" the players because of the increasing level of tension and distrust.

18. Don't overuse the word "don't" in coaching players. Remember, the brain doesn't know the meaning of "don't." Top performing coaches always stress what "to do" rather than harping on what "not to do." The legendary basketball coach John Wooden had his coaching performance studied by two researchers from a college for an entire year. To their amazement, the overwhelming majority of his comments and coaching were preceded by the phrase "do this" and seldom "don't do this." (Please waive the advice for the item you've just read, which, of course, begins with "don't.")

24.

Gamebreakers for Fans

Thanksgiving dinners take 18 hours to prepare. They are consumed in 12 minutes. Halftimes take 12 minutes. This is not a coincidence.

— **Erma Bombeck, humorist**

All right. We've beaten up on players and coaches. Now it's time to look at some stuff that can get you in trouble as a fan. Here are the rookie mistakes you need to try to avoid:

1. Fixating on the ball. Fans miss much of the game because they too often watch the ball: where it is run, passed and kicked. Football is one of the great team games with 22 players doing very specific things during any football play. Resist the temptation to watch the football at all times; otherwise, you'll miss a lot of the "inner game."

When you watch an actor deliver his or her lines, it's sometimes worthwhile to take your eyes off them and watch the other actors to see how they react to those lines. A river guide will take his eyes off the immediate scene and gaze ahead, taking in the challenges and peril to come. In the same way, use your vision to look beyond the ball: what is the pass defense doing while the quarterback drops back to pass? Is everyone covered? Do you see someone open, without being covered? Who would you throw to? All this before the pass is thrown.

By the way, occasionally keep your eyes on the quarterback after he passes, particularly when he gets a heavy rush. You'll see the physical pounding he can take from pass rushers who can't, or won't, stop the instant the ball is thrown. Many miss this, including those directing TV coverage, who follow the ball as it is thrown and don't appreciate how rough the game can be for the quarterback.

2. Not paying attention to down and distance. Coaches in the press box chart what each team does on every play by down and distance. They want to know what the other team is doing on first down. Are they balanced with run and pass? Are they giving clues as to what they may try? The distance for a first down is important because defensive coaches predict what the offense will try to do and call a defense accordingly. It's fun for fans to predict what kind of plays teams are going to try before the ball is snapped. If you guess wrong, don't worry; just keep track of what they did do and use that for your next prediction.

3. Not paying attention to field position. Teams will do certain things in parts of the field and not in others. A team will probably not pass on fourth-and-one to go or run on third-and-20. Understand that as teams get closer to their opponent's goal line, they can afford to gamble more, in part because they have an extra play since they don't need to punt — "four-down territory" — and in part because a fumble or interception isn't as deadly. As the game goes on, try predicting what kind of play, pass or run, the offense will do based on down, distance and its location on the field.

4. Taking a play for granted. The terminology for this unforgiveable sin by players is called "taking a play off," meaning the player does not pay attention or try his best. As a fan, you can take a play off, too, but while the player will be blasted by his coach for doing so, you only might miss the most important play of the game. Maintain your concentration, and use your timeouts wisely.

5. Losing your focus. It's natural to carry on conversations with your fellow fans during the game. If you're hearing what your best friend's daughter is going to wear at her upcoming wedding, you're distracted; keep your eyes on the game and your ongoing process of observation and evaluation. You don't need to look at her to hear her conversation! You are becoming a real pro when you can hear an unrelated conversation while watching the game and you don't miss anything. After all, that's why they have breaks between quarters and halftime. (Although the experienced fan will probably want to compare his/her observations with other spectators, particularly those who don't seem too drunk or out of control). At some point, you're going to realize you're getting more out of the the game than most everyone else around you.

6. Depending too much on television commentators. Realize that many of the commentators on television are telling you what's happening and will point out particular parts of the game, but they are not invested in helping you learn the game through your own eyes. You can't depend on them or the cameras to totally reveal the game. When replays are shown, watch the players in the background: are they holding someone? Who's missing tackles? Why and what do you think is happening? Never mind the blather of the commentator who might still be suffering from the concussion he picked up back when he was a player.

25.

Your Final 'Game Plan'

Look at a football field. It looks like a big movie screen. This is theatre. Football combines the strategy of chess. It's part ballet. It's part battleground, part playground. We clarify, amplify and glorify the game with our footage, the narration and that music, and in the end create an inspirational piece of footage.

— **Steve Sabol, NFL Films**

When a football team comes onto the field to start a game, the offense and defense have very specific game plans: *Here's what we're going to do to give us the best chance to win.* If you want to enjoy watching football to the max, here's a game plan for you:

1. Opening kickoff: Don't watch the ball. Watch the middle five players on the kickoff team run down the field trying to avoid opposing players attempting to block them. It's going to look like a mob breaking through a police barrier. Try and find the two fastest players and remember to watch them on another kickoff. Did anyone get knocked down?

2. First offensive play: Don't watch the ball. Catch that on the replay. Watch the offensive linemen come off the ball when it's snapped to the quarterback: if it was a run, did they push the defensive line backwards? If it was a pass, were they able to protect the quarterback?

3. Second offensive play: Don't watch the ball. Watch the defensive linemen this time. Does it look like they're attacking the offensive linemen in front of them? Do they look strong? Are they getting pushed around?

4. Third offensive play: Don't watch the ball. Watch the defensive backs. Are they talking or signaling to each other? Does it look like they are reacting quickly, with confidence? Does it look like they want to help make the tackle?

5. First Punt: Don't watch the ball. Watch the two outside gunners — the end men on the line of the punt team. Are they able to break free from players trying to hold them up and block them? Do they look fast? Are they able to get close to the punt returner before the ball gets there? If you can, check the returner. Did he catch the ball with confidence? If he was able to get a runback, did he look quick or show some elusive running moves?

6. Play selection on first down: Does the offense seem to favor running the ball or passing the ball on first down? Four yards or more gained on first down is considered success; is the offense consistently gaining that much?

7. Play selection on second down: Again, is there a favored choice between run and pass? How many times does the offense face a second-and-more-than-6-yards situation? If the number grows, an inverse relationship begins to fester because the odds of the defense forcing a punt or turnover increase.

8. Play selection on third down: Does the offense face a short or medium-yardage choice — four or fewer yards to go — or a long-yardage choice — five or more yards to go? Try and keep track. Offenses that find themselves consistently in long-yardage situations on third down usually have to punt and give the ball back to the defense more than 50-60 percent of the time.

9. Second punt: Watch the inside five linemen blocking on the punt team. Do they retreat a bit before releasing down the field? Are they being held up by members of the punt-return team? If you were the defensive coach, do you think your players might be able to get past the blockers and block a punt later in the game?

10. Offensive plays: Watch the offensive line three plays in a row. Can you tell if the line is successful blocking the defense? Does any offensive lineman stand out to you? Does one team's center look better than the other team's?

11. Defensive plays: After watching the offensive line three plays in a row, do the same for the defensive line. Again, does any one player stand out?

12. More defensive plays: Watch the linebackers react and run to the ball for several plays. Are they active in both run and pass defense? Do you see any one player around the ball more than others? Does it look like the offense is trying to stay away from a particular defensive player?

13. Pass plays: Watch to see the defensive pass rush. How many players are coming? If it's more than four, it's a blitz and the pass defense may be a bit weaker. Are the pass rushers getting close to the quarterback?

14. More pass plays: What does the offense try to do when it passes? Is the team throwing long or short passes? Does it look like the quarterback has a favorite receiver? Who does he throw to on third down?

15. More punts: Are the players covering for the punting team getting down the field fast? Are you beginning to see more of them in your vision? As your vision expands you will also begin to see the whole team running down the field to tackle the return man. Can you anticipate a return opening up for big yardage?

16. More kickoffs: Continue to watch the interior five on the coverage team as they run down the field. Does the return team do anything different while trying to block its opponent?

17. More kickoffs: Are the blockers who form in front of the return man running the same direction each kick, or are they running up the sideline? Does it look like they are blocking well enough to spring the return man for big yardage? Are you seeing any blockers who look like they are afraid and don't want to hit anyone?

18. Offense: Watch the running backs and quarterback at the same time. Are they executing their assignments smoothly? Do they show confidence?

19. Big play, either team: Watch a team that gives up a big play and/or score to see how the team reacts. Are the players coming off the field showing any emotion or energy? How do the coaches react to this adversity? Are they angry or trying to be positive and supportive of their players? Ask yourself the same questions if it was the offense giving up the big play: how and what are the reactions of players and coaches? Does it look positive or negative?

20. Another big play, either team: In regard to a defensive team that makes the big play — how does the offensive team react? What do the players show you coming off the field? What is the reaction of their coaches?

21. Goal line (ball on three-yard line or closer): Watch the pass receivers lined up and the pass patterns they run. Did they try a pick play or a fade? Do you see a short pass defender trying to guard a tall wide receiver?

As time ticks to a close in this book, let me ask: Are you getting a better sense of how to watch a football game?

As you step into the world of football, don't be afraid to make mistakes. You're not going to learn all this at once. It took me 18 years — and I'm still learning. It will help if you're sitting next to someone who's willing to listen to what you say you're seeing. It might actually lead to more enjoyment for them, too; but if there's no one there, just repeat it to yourself.

Repetition is a must in learning a new skill and reminding your brain what you are seeing each play will make you a knowledgeable football fan. The more football you watch, the smarter you'll get, equating to fun, guaranteed. And now, you have a lot more information on how to watch football with confidence.

Until reading this book, you might have wondered why football has been called America's Greatest Game. With what you've learned in this book, you'll have the opportunity of finding out for yourself as the game plays out on a 100-yard-long stage in front of you. Just remember: from time to time, take your eyes off the ball.

"I love sport because I love life, and sport is one of the basic joys of life."

— Yevgeny Yevtushenko, poet

Glossary of terms

That boy didn't know the meaning of the word fear. In fact, I just saw his grades, and that boy don't know the meaning of a lot of words.
— **Bobby Bowden, coach, Florida State**

A

all purpose yardage — The total yards gained by a player on offense rushing and receiving yards; on defense, yards on returns of interceptions and fumbles; and in the kicking game, yards on kickoffs, punts and runbacks of missed field goal returns.

attempt — An offensive "try" by a player. Three kinds: a pass, a rush and a place kick.

audible — At the line of scrimmage, the act of a quarterback signaling, verbally or with hand signals, to change the play initially called in the huddle or at the line of scrimmage. Defenses do the same, referred to as a "check."

automatic first down — A fresh set of four downs offered to the offensive team in cases of severe fouls committed by the defensive team. This is awarded even if the result of the penalty yardage does not result in such. In both pro and college football, the fouls include pass interference, defensive holding and all personal fouls.

B

backfield — On offense, the area of the field behind the linemen on the line of scrimmage. "Backfield" can also refer to all offensive players aligned behind the line, such as the quarterback, running back and fullback. On defense, the cornerbacks and safeties.

backup — A player who does not start the beginning of the game on offense or defense.

backward pass — A pass thrown backward or sideways, technically a "lateral." There is no limit to the number of backward passes that can be thrown on any one play, or where they may be thrown from and to whom they may be thrown.

ball control — An offensive strategy based on low-risk plays to maintain possession of the ball and to maximize their time of possession, often to protect a late-game lead.

bean bag — An item thrown by a referee to mark the spot of a fumble that occurs before the play is whistled dead.

blind side — The side of the quarterback opposite his throwing arm. A right-handed passer's blind side is to his left because, as he sets to throw, he can't see pass rushers coming from that direction.

blitz — The defense rushing the passer with five or more players. Linebackers are the primary blitzers although safeties and, occasionally, a cornerback will be called into the rush.

block — An offensive player obstructing a defender with his body, either pushing the opponent back or shielding him from the ball carrier.

blocking back — A running back assigned to block for a single play or a back's primary function in the offense.

block in the back — A 10-yard penalty for blocking a defender above the waist from behind. Usually occurs during kicking plays when defenders react unpredictably.

blowout — A game in which one team beats the other by a whole lot of points.

bomb — A long, high pass, usually along the sideline to a fast receiver. Also called a "long bomb."

bootleg — A misdirected offensive play in which the quarterback pretends to hand the ball to a player going in one direction, then carries the ball in the opposite direction, then either passes or runs. In early football, the quarterback would put the ball on his hip to hide it, much like a bootlegger would sneak a whiskey flask past a policeman during Prohibition.

box — An area on the defensive side of the ball, directly opposite the offensive linemen and about 5 yards deep. The area of the offensive formation the defense needs to defend to stop the running attack.

bubble screen — A screen pass where the quarterback takes the snap and immediately throws to a wide receiver lined up to the far right or left, protected by one or more receivers lined up on the same side of the field and a guard and tackle who are pulling to help block.

bump and run — A strategy in which a defensive back plays close to the receiver, bumping him when he tries to release and then runs with him, man-to-man.

busted play — An offensive play that deteriorates and leads to chaos on the field because of a blown assignment, technique error, players going in the wrong direction or a surprise move by the defense.

buttonhook (hook, dig) — Pass route in which a receiver runs straight up field, stops hard, and turns back toward the quarterback to receive the ball.

C

carry or carries — A statistic referring to the number of times a rushing player attempts to run the ball.

center — An offensive lineman in the center of the formation who snaps the ball to the quarterback and blocks defensive men, often after setting blocking responsibilities for the rest of the line.

center-eligible — A trick play where the entire offensive line is to one side of the center at the snap, so that the center is an extra lineman on the end, and therefore an eligible receiver.

chain — The device used by the three-man sideline "chain gang" to measure the 10-yard distance required by the offense to earn a first down.

check down pass — A pass in which the quarterback, after looking at deeper receivers who are covered, throws a short pass to a running back or tight end as his last choice to avoid a sack.

chip shot — A short field goal or extra point kick, named after the golf term for the ball's high and short trajectory, that is almost certain to be successful; an easy kick.

chop block — A 15-yard penalty called when, simultaneously, one offensive player blocks a defensive player below the knees and another offensive player blocks him above the waist. The penalty attempts to prevent knee and ankle injuries.

clipping — A 15-yard penalty in which a defensive player is blocked from the back at or below the waist by an offensive player.

coffin corner — The corner of the field of play between the end zone and the 5-yard line where a punter will attempt to kick the ball out of bounds to put the offense in poor field position.

comeback route — A receiver's pass route in which he runs straight upfield, driving the defender deep, plants hard, then turns back towards the sideline at a 45-degree angle. The quarterback will throw the ball two to three yards short of the receiver's cut to force him to come back for, and shield the defender from, the ball.

contain — A defensive tactic to deny the runner getting around end and forcing him to turn inside towards the pursuing defenders.

cornerback (CB) — A defensive back who often positions himself near the line of scrimmage, across from a wide receiver, to guard receivers and to contain the runner on rushing plays aimed to go around the ends.

cover — To prevent a pass receiver from catching a pass or to prevent a kick or punt receiver from advancing the ball.

counter — An offensive play in which the running back takes a step in one direction, only to reverse his direction and take the hand-off going the other.

crack-back block — An illegal block delivered below the opponent's waist by an offensive player who enters the neutral zone of blocking from the outside. Also a legal block, delivered by a wide receiver without leaving his feet, from the front, or side, on a defender inside of him.

cut — A sharp change of direction by a running player.

cut blocking — A blocking technique in which offensive linemen, and sometimes others, block legally below the waist to knock down a defender.

D

dead ball — The act of the referee blowing his whistle to declare a play over.

dead-ball foul — A penalty committed by either team before or after a play is in process. A frequent example is delay of game or illegal procedure on the offense.

defensive back (DB) — A cornerback or safety on the defensive team, primarily charged with pass defense against receivers.

defensive end (DE) — A player on defense who lines up on the outside of the line and whose job is to pressure the quarterback, force running plays to the inside of the field and, of course, tackle runners.

defensive tackle (DT) — A player on defense who lines up on the inside of the defensive line and whose principal responsibility is to defend inside running plays and to rush the quarterback on pass plays.

defensive team — The team that begins a play from scrimmage without the ball, defending the offense against scoring points.

delay of game — A 5-yard penalty that occurs when the offensive team does not put the ball in play before the 40-second play clock runs out. And, infrequently, a 5-yard penalty called when a defensive player holds an offensive player on the ground to prevent him from lining up, often as time is running short.

dime defensive back — The second extra, or sixth total, defensive back who substitutes in for a lineman in long-yardage passing situations.

dink and dunk — Pass offense predicated on short, simple routes in front of the defensive backs.

direct snap — An offensive play in which the ball is passed from the center directly to a player who then runs, passes or hands off. Often referred to as a "wildcat" formation when a running back receives the snap and runs the ball.

dive — A play in which the ball is handed off to a running back, who rushes through the middle of the defense between the offensive guard and tackle.

double reverse — A play in which the ball reverses direction twice behind the line of scrimmage. Often consists of the quarterback running one way, handing to a running back going the other, who then pitches or hands off to a wide receiver going the opposite direction.

double wing — A formation with a tight end and a wingback on each side of a balanced formation.

down — A unit of the game that starts with a legal snap or legal free kick after the ball is ruled ready for play and ends when the play is over and the ball is ruled dead.

down box — The vertical indicator, usually black with orange numbers, used by the "chain gang" to mark the line of scrimmage and designate the current down — 1, 2, 3 or 4.

down by contact — When the ball carrier touches the ground with any part of his body other than his feet, hands or arms as a direct result of contact with a player of the opposing team. In professional football a player must be down by contact in order for play to stop; if he falls without being touched by an opposing player he is free to get up and continue advancing the ball. Not so in college. When you're down, you're down, even if you slipped.

down lineman — A player stationed on the line of scrimmage and who has either one (three-point stance) or two (four-point stance) hands on the ground.

draw play — A play in which the quarterback drops back as if to pass, then hands off to a running back or runs with the ball himself, "drawing" the rush of the defenders in hopes they'll run past the ball carrier and leave the inside lane open.

drive — A continuous set of offensive plays gaining substantial yardage and several first downs, often leading to a scoring opportunity.

drive block — A move in which an offensive lineman powerfully drives the defender from a head-on position straight back off the line of scrimmage, opening a hole for the running back.

dual threat quarterback — A quarterback skilled at both passing and rushing the ball.

E

eligible receivers — Offensive players who may legally touch a forward pass, provided the player's jersey displays a number in the ranges allowed for eligible receivers: 1-49 and 80-99. All players of the defensive team are eligible to receive a pass (see "interception") and once the ball is touched by a defensive player, even formerly ineligible offensive receivers may touch — and catch and advance — the ball.

encroachment — An illegal action by a defensive player in which a player crosses the neutral zone and makes contact with an opponent before the ball is snapped, resulting in a 5-yard penalty.

end around — An offensive play in which the quarterback hands the ball off to an in-motion wide receiver who heads to the opposite side of the field from which he began.

end zone — The area between the end line and the goal line, bounded by the sidelines; 10 yards deep in American football. (Interestingly, end zones in Canadian football are 25 yards deep.)

extra points — From the 3-yard line (college) or the 15-yard-line (pro), an attempt at a single point scored after a touchdown by a kicker kicking the ball through the goalposts. Or, from the 3-yard-line (college) or the 2-yard-line (pros), a successful run or pass play for two points.

F

face-mask penalty — A foul in which a player grabs the face mask or helmet-opening of another player's helmet, usually in the process of making a tackle. Penalty: 15 yards. Or, if ruled accidental, 10 yards.

false start — A foul, resulting in a 5-yard penalty, in which an offensive player moves before the ball is snapped, potentially drawing defensive players offside.

fair catch — An unhindered catch of an opponent's punt or kickoff by a player who holds up an arm to signal "don't tackle me!" The player catching the ball can't be touched by an opponent, nor can he advance the ball once he's caught it or attempt to block an opponent.

field judge — The official who keeps the game time on the field.

field goal — A score of three points made by place- or drop-kicking the ball — rare! — through the opponent's goal other than via a kickoff or free kick following a safety. A missed, or blocked, field goal can be returned as a punt, if recovered in-bounds by the defending team. If a scrimmage kick is blocked and the ball does not cross the neutral zone, all players are eligible to pick it up and run with it.

field position — A relative measure of how many yards a team must travel in order to score. "Good field position" for an offense would be taking possession at midfield after a punt. "Bad field position" would be an offensive team starting from inside its own 10-yard-line.

first down — The initial play in a set of four downs. Also, a new set of four downs awarded to an offensive team that advances the ball 10 yards in four plays or fewer.

flag — A weighted yellow cloth thrown by a field official to indicate a foul has been committed. Sometimes officials will toss another item on the field for other reasons. For example, when a receiver without the ball goes out of bounds, an official will toss his hat at the spot to indicate such, meaning that unless the player was forced out of bounds by an opposing player, he is ineligible to return to the field and catch a pass.

flanker — An offensive wide receiver (Z receiver) who lines up in the backfield outside of another receiver.

flat — On defense, the outside area of the field between the line of scrimmage and 10 yards deep into the defensive backfield, within 15 yards of the sideline.

flea flicker — A trick play in which a running back takes the handoff from the quarterback, stops and throws a backward pass back to the QB, who then throws a pass to a receiver deep down the field.

formation — The set-up of the offense or defense. On offense, a formation usually is described in terms of how the running backs line up or how the wide receivers line up (e.g. "trips left," in which three wide receivers line up to the left of the linemen).

forward pass — A pass that touches a player, official or the ground closer to the opponent's end line than from where it was released.

forward progress — The location to which a ball carrier's forward momentum carries him before he is tackled or deemed down by the officials, even if he is pushed back by the defenders or never touches the ground.

fourth down — The final in a set of four downs. Teams doubting that they can make the necessary yardage for a first down often punt on fourth down or, if within range, attempt a field goal.

fourth-down conversion — The act of using a fourth down play to make a first down, commonly called "going for it." Rare unless (a) the amount of yardage needed for the conversion is small (a yard or less); (b) the team is trailing by a significant amount with time running out; (c) a team is too far away to realistically make a field goal but too close for a punt to be practical; or (d) in overtime, when a team must score to win or tie to extend the game.

four-down territory — That part of the field where the offense feels it can risk turning the ball over to the defense if it doesn't get a first down, usually on the defense's side of the 50-yard line. Or when the offense is behind and must score to have a chance to win.

four-point stance — An offensive or defensive lineman's stance with four points on the ground: two feet and two hands.

free kick — A kick made to put the ball in play with a place kick or punt following a safety or fair catch.

free safety (FS) — A defensive back who is primarily responsible for covering the middle of the secondary, assisting other defensive backs in deep coverage.

front four — The defensive line; also used to describe a "normal" pass rush.

fullback (FB) — An offensive back lined up behind the quarterback in the T or I formation. Bigger because he has more blocking responsibilities than other backs, he is usually the slowest player in the backfield.

fumble — A situation in which a player with the football loses possession of the ball, either by his mishandling of it or a defender's contact.

G

goal posts — For field goal and extra-point kicking attempts, two upright posts extending above a horizontal crossbar the top edge of which is 10 feet off the ground. The width between each pole is 18 feet, 6 inches for college and pro football, and 23 feet, 4 inches for high school football. The goal is above the bar and between the edges of the posts, centered above each end line of the end zone, usually topped with marking ribbons showing the prevailing wind direction.

goal line —The front of the end zone, marking the "promised land," the scoring goal of every offensive team. It often is designated by a stripe that's slightly thicker than the other white yard lines.

goal line stand — One team's defense stopping another team's offense from scoring a touchdown when the ball is close to the goal line, often resulting in an emotional lift to the team that accomplished it.

guard (OG) — One of two offensive linemen, each of whom lines up on either side of the center.

gunslinger — Quarterback who plays in an aggressive and decisive manner by throwing deep, risky and often successful passes.

gunner —Widest player on either side of a punt formation. The gunner is often one of the fastest players on the team, whose responsibility it is to down the punt if it is not caught or to make the return man hold up, attempting to evade his tackle.

H

Hail Mary — As time is running out at the end of the first half or the game, a long, desperation pass thrown toward a group of receivers near or in the end zone in hopes of a touchdown or pass interference penalty. Referring to a Catholic prayer, it was first coined after the Dallas Cowboys' last-second win over the Minnesota Vikings in 1975.

halfback (HB) — An offensive player who lines up in the backfield, or is a type of defensive back. The offensive back who lines up directly behind the quarterback is called a tailback.

halfback option — A trick play in which the halfback, after taking the ball from the quarterback and while sweeping left or right, throws a pass.

half the distance — On a distance penalty, the yardage enforced from a spot so near the offending team's own goal line that instead of having to take the full amount of yardage the team only loses half the yardage between that spot and the goal line. For example, a team at its own 6-yard-line that's whistled for an illegal shift would, instead of being penalized 5 yards and having the ball placed at the 1-yard-line, would get the ball at the 3-yard-line.

handoff — A move in which a player transfers the ball to another player directly, usually a quarterback giving the ball to a running back.

hands team — When an onside kick is a strong possibility, a group of players on the receiving team who are used to handling the football (wide receivers, offensive backs) and who are placed on the front lines to make sure the ball is recovered.

hard count — A strategy commonly used by offenses to draw the defense offside with the quarterback dramatically altering his regular snap count with sudden sharp inflections in critical short-yardage situations.

hash marks — Lines, or white dashes, on the playing surface — one yard apart — between which the ball is spotted to begin each play, even if the proceeding play ended outside them. As such, the two sets of marks delineate a rough "middle of the field," 40 feet wide in college. The ball is spotted where it is blown dead unless the play ends outside the hash marks, in which case it's placed at the nearest hash mark.

h back — A player listed as a fullback or tight end who has good athletic or pass-catching abilities and plays as a hybrid of a running back and a tight end.

hike — Known as the "snap," the handoff or pass from the center that begins a play from scrimmage.

holder — A player who holds the ball upright for a place kick and, in rare cases, will, instead, attempt a run or pass for a two-point conversion.

holding — An infraction in which an offensive player illegally

Jerry Thompson

The player in white may be doing his best to block the defender but if a referee were to catch his effort the result would be a 10-yard penalty for holding.

blocks a defensive player by grabbing and holding his uniform or body (10-yard penalty). Conversely, a defensive player holding an offensive player who's not actively making an attempt to catch the ball. 10-yard penalty, automatic first down.

hook and ladder — A trick play in which a wide receiver runs a hook pattern and, after the catch, laterals to a second player going in a different direction, usually catching defenders by surprise.

horse-collar tackle — An illegal tackle in which a defender grabs the back-inside of an opponent's shoulder pads or jersey. Made illegal in 2008, it carries a 15-yard personal foul penalty.

hot read — When a quarterback sees a blitz coming and quickly passes to a receiver running a short route.

huddle — An on-field formation of team members to communicate instructions for the up-coming play.

hurry-up offense — An offensive strategy designed to gain as much yardage as possible while running as little time off the clock as possible, often without a huddle to keep the defense off-balance.

I

I formation — An offensive setup that features a fullback in front of the tailback, both lined up directly behind a quarterback who takes the snap directly from the center.

icing the kicker — A desperate ploy the coach of a team on defense might use to psychologically "freeze" an opponent's field goal kicker. To do so, he calls timeout just before the ball is snapped, usually before a last-second, potential game-tying or game-winning field goal. It rarely works.

illegal formation — An offensive setup that does not consist of the requisite number of men on the line of scrimmage (minimum of seven) for at least one count before the ball is snapped. 5-yard penalty.

illegal motion — On offense, an infraction that occurs when a player behind the line of scrimmage, prior to the snap, goes in motion forward instead of laterally or backward. 5-yard penalty.

illegal shift — On offense, an infraction when more than one player goes in motion. Only one player is allowed to be in pre-snap motion. Another may do so but, like the first person who shifts, must be in the "set" position for one second before the snap. 5-yard penalty.

incidental contact — Contact between a receiver and defender that is not sufficient enough to result in a penalty. Both have a right to go for the football, and bumping contact is allowed if it's "incidental," meaning each is making a "bona fide" attempt to reach for the ball.

incomplete pass — A forward pass that no player catches.

ineligible receiver — Lineman who can't legally catch passes. Linemen numbered 50-79 are not allowed to catch passes — unless the ball has been tipped by an eligible offensive receiver or any defender.

intentional grounding — An illegal forward pass, thrown without a receiver in the area, to conserve time or avoid a sack and loss of yardage. Penalty: Loss of down and 10 yards, though if the foul is committed in the end zone, the result is a safety. Intentional grounding is not called in the case of a "spike," a ball thrown directly to the turf to stop the clock.

interception — The legal catching of a forward pass thrown by an opposing player.

interference — The blockers in advance of the ball carrier in the open field; not to be confused with "pass interference."

J

jam — When a defender uses his hands, legally, to delay a receiver at the line of scrimmage.

jumbo — An offensive formation designed for maximum size and power that includes two tight ends, a fullback and perhaps an extra lineman in a goal line or short yardage situation.

K

kick —A punt or place kick.

kicker or place kicker (PK) — Player who specializes in place kicking field goals and/or kickoffs.

kickoff — A free kick that starts each half or restarts the game following a touchdown or field goal. The kickoff may be a place kick or, rarely in modern days, a drop kick.

kick-out block — When a pulling guard or running back blocks the end man on the line of scrimmage towards the sideline, creating a lane inside the guard's block for the running back.

kick returner — A player on the receiving team who catches, and returns, kicks.

kick six — A field goal attempt or punt that is blocked and returned for a touchdown by the defense.

kneel — A low-risk play in which the player in possession of the ball kneels down after receiving the snap, ending the play while keeping the clock running. Usually used by a team that is ahead at the end of either half.

L

lateral — See "backward pass."

leg whip —A dangerous, illegal block or tackle using the legs to trip the opponent. 15-yard penalty.

line of scrimmage — The line running parallel to the neutral zone between the offensive and defensive teams from where the ball is snapped before each play.

linebacker (LB) — A defensive position in which the defender plays 1 to 6 yards behind the defensive linemen and has responsibilities for both runs and passes.

lineman — Defensive and offensive players who face each other on the line of scrimmage.

live ball — Any ball that is in play and can be recovered by either team. The ball is live during plays from scrimmage, kickoffs (once the ball travels 10 yards) and free kicks.

live-ball foul — A foul assessed for various infractions such as changing numbers while the ball is in play.

long snapper — A center who specializes in the long snaps required for punts and field goal attempts.

loose ball — Any ball that is in play and is not in a player's possession. This includes a ball in flight during a backward or forward pass.

M

man in motion — A player on offense who's moving backward or parallel to the line of scrimmage at the snap. Only one offensive player can be in motion at a time and cannot be moving toward the line of scrimmage at the snap.

man-to-man coverage — A defense in which linebackers and defensive backs cover a specific offensive receiver.

Marty ball — A conservative game plan that involves an offense based around the use of running backs with use of the passing game only to advance the running game, and a great emphasis on defense. Popular term for Marty Schottenheimer's approach to coaching.

maximum protection — A modification used on pass plays that keeps the tight end and both backs in behind the line of scrimmage to protect the quarterback instead of running pass routes.

mesh point — Term for the split-second moment when the quarterback puts the ball on the stomach of a running back, either handing it off or keeping it, depending on the defensive reaction.

Mike (MLB) — The middle linebacker in a 4-3 formation and in the 3-4 formation, the interior linebacker who plays on the strong side of the formation. Name can change, but it will always start with an "M" for "middle."

monster man (SS) — On defense, the strong safety in a secondary with the responsibility to cover deep zones, defend against runs and, on occasion, play on the line of scrimmage.

motion — The ordered movement of eligible receivers off the line of scrimmage, only one player a time, prior to the snap.

muff —A loose ball, after kickoff or punt, that's dropped or mishandled while the player is attempting to gain possession. The defensive team can recover but not advance a muff.

N

naked bootleg — When the quarterback fakes to a running back going one way and rolls out the other way, without any blocking protection, to run or throw.

neutral zone —The area between the lines of scrimmage or between the free-kick restraining lines.

nickel back — An extra, or fifth, defensive back utilized in passing situations. Named after the coin, worth five cents.

no-huddle offense — A tactic where the offense quickly forms on the line of scrimmage immediately after a play, without a formal "gathering."

nose tackle —A tackle in a three-man defensive line who lines up opposite the center. He's called that because he is aligned on the center's nose.

O

offensive team —The team with possession of the ball.

offside — An infraction that occurs, at the snap, when a player from either team moves across the line dividing the offense from the defense. 5-yard penalty.

one-back formation — A formation in which the offensive team has only one running back in the backfield with the quarterback.

onside kick — A play in which the kicking team tries to recover a deliberately short kickoff once the ball has gone at least 10 yards and, thus, has become "live" for either team to claim.

open — When an intended receiver, usually through speed and/or change of direction, is separated from defenders and in good position to catch a pass.

option —A play in which the quarterback can choose to hand off, keep the ball himself or pass, depending on how the defense is aligned and, once the ball is snapped, is pursuing.

option offense — An offense that relies predominantly on option plays. (See "option.")

overtime — An extra period of time extending the game to determine a winner in the event of a tie score.

P

PAT —Point after touchdown, same as "try" or "extra point."

package — The group of players on the field for a specific situation, usually determined by down and distance. Example: A nickel "package" substitutes a fifth cornerback for a linebacker or defensive lineman in passing situations.

pancake block — When a defensive player is knocked to the ground by a blocker, flattening him like a pancake.

pass — An action performed by an offensive player who throws the ball to an eligible player, numbered 1-49 or 80-99. Every pass is either a forward pass or a lateral pass, depending on its direction.

pass interference — An infraction, also known as "PI," when a player illegally hinders an eligible receiver's opportunity to catch a forward pass. In college: 15-yard penalty and automatic first down; in pros, automatic first down at point of infraction.

pass protection — Pass blocking by the offensive line, tight ends and backs to protect the quarterback from being sacked, and to allow him time and space to throw the ball.

passer rating or quarterback rating — A numeric rating, used to measure the performance of quarterbacks, involving the player's completion percentage, passing yards, touchdowns and interceptions.

passing yards — The distance in total yards gained from scrimmage that a passer has thrown the football plus the distance any receivers have run after catching the ball.

peel-back block — An action where an offensive player blocks a defender who is moving back toward his own end zone. The blocks are illegal below the waist and from either the back or the side. The blocker must avoid "unnecessary force" as recent rules recognize the defender doesn't see what is coming, is in a "defenseless" position and is vulnerable to injury.

pick —The use of an offensive player to screen a defender by impeding his course of movement to allow a receiver to get open. This is usually done by design but can occur accidentally when receivers try to avoid defensive backs. Also, slang name for an interception.

pick-six — An interception that is run back for a touchdown and, thus, six points.

pistol formation — A hybrid version of the shotgun in which the quarterback lines up about three yards behind the center and the running back lines up directly behind the quarterback.

place kick — Kicking the ball from where it has been placed and held on the ground by another player.

play action — A pass play in which the quarterback fakes a run handoff to draw the defense away from the receiver, then throws to a receiver open by virtue of the run fake.

play clock — A timer used to increase the pace of the game between plays. College teams have 40 seconds to start the new play after the previous play is ruled dead or receive a 5-yard penalty for delay of game.

pocket — An area on the offensive side of the line of scrimmage, shaped like a cup, where the offensive linemen attempt to prevent defensive players from reaching the quarterback on pass plays.

pooch kick — A short punt or kickoff that is deliberately kicked with less than full force, intended, on a punt, to pin a team deep in its own territory and, on a kickoff, to prevent a speedy returner from getting the ball.

position — A place where a player plays relative to teammates. Also, a player's individual responsibility on the team.

possession — Physical control of the ball after a catch, handoff or fumble.

post pattern — A passing route in which the receiver sprints approximately 8 to 10 yards, fakes a look back at the quarterback as he sprints deep toward the middle of the field, in the direction of the goal posts.

prevent defense — A defensive strategy that, with a team's willingness to give up shorter passes, utilizes deep zone coverage in order to prevent long passes.

pro set — Offensive formation using two backs, lined up side-by-side two or three yards behind a quarterback, who takes a direct snap from center.

pulling — The act of an offensive lineman who, instead of blocking the player in front of him, steps back from the line (pulls) and runs to block a defender outside of his original position.

pump fake — The act of a quarterback faking a pass to a receiver, attempting to fool the defensive back into committing to the short route, and then throwing a long pass.

punt — A kick in which the ball is dropped by a player and kicked before it reaches the ground. Used to return the ball to the opposition after an offense has not made a first down after three plays in a series.

punt return — When a punt is fielded by the receiving team and advanced for better field position. The punt returner attempts to run the ball as far as possible or signals for a fair catch, which gives him an unimpeded chance to catch the ball with no return.

punter (P) — A kicker who specializes in punting.

pylon — Orange plastic marker planted in the four corners of each end zone. If a ball carrier, on his feet or in the air, contacts the ball with a pylon on the goal line, the result is a touchdown.

Q

quarter — One of four periods of play in a football game. A quarter lasts for 15 game-clock minutes in college and pro games and 12 minutes in high school.

quarterback (QB) — An offensive player who lines up behind the center and takes the snap to begin the play. He is considered the on-field leader of the offense.

quarterback sneak — A play used in ultra-short-yardage or goal-line situations, often on quick counts to catch the defense off guard. QB takes the snap directly behind center and follows his block up the middle.

quarter defense — A defensive formation with seven defensive backs, three down linemen and one linebacker.

quick kick —An unexpected punt, usually by the quarterback, kicked from a regular offensive formation on any down but fourth, designed to surprise the defense and prevent a punt return.

R

read — Just prior to the snap, the mental interpretation of an opposing player's probable reaction at the snap of the ball. Every player on both offense and defense has one or more "reads" to help him decide what to do once the play begins.

reception — When an offensive player catches the ball beyond the line of scrimmage.

red flag — A weighted red marker thrown onto the field by a coach to tell the officials that he wants a certain play reviewed; sometimes referred to as a "challenge flag."

red shirt —A college player who, though practicing, is forgoing a season by not playing in any games to retain a year of eligibility. After they enroll, student athletes have five years to play four football seasons — except in rare cases of medical hardship.

red zone — The area between the 20-yard line and the goal line of the defensive team that's considered, for statistical purposes, to be "scoring territory." Potent offensive teams will have a high red-zone percentage based on their making lots of touchdowns or field goals when reaching this area — which, by the way, is not literally outlined in red on the field.

referee — The head official who directs the other seven officials on the field.

restraining line — A team's respective line of scrimmage. Also, on a free kick, for the kicking team, the line the ball is to be kicked from or, for the receiving team, the line 10 yards in advance of that line.

return — Catching and running with a kick, pass interception or fumble recovery.

return yards — Yards gained advancing the ball during play after a change of possession on a punt or kickoff — or on a turnover after a fumble or interception.

reverse — An offensive play in which a running back carries the ball toward one side of the field and hands or tosses the ball to a teammate who is running in the opposite direction.

rover — A hybrid safety who has dual responsibilities as a defensive back and a linebacker, the same as strong safety or monster in other teams' schemes.

run and shoot — An offensive philosophy designed to force the defense to show its hand prior to the snap of the ball after the "O" splits up receivers and sends them in motion.

running back (RB) — A player position on offense whose chief responsibility is taking handoffs from the quarterback and running.

running out the clock — A late-game strategy used by the team ahead involving the use of maximum amount of time possible and safe, simple rushing plays. It's a wise way to keep the ball away from the other team and to ensure victory.

running up the score — A generally discouraged practice in which a team, despite winning by an insurmountable margin, continues to try and score in an attempt to inflate their own egos, embarrass the opposition or both. Can backfire in subsequent years as opponents "get even."

rush —An attempt to tackle or hurry a player before he can throw a pass or make a kick. Also a running play.

rushing average or **yards per carry average** — The quotient of a player's total rushing yards divided by the number of rushing attempts. Better running backs will average in the 5-to 9-yard range.

S

sack — A statistical category for defensive players who earn one for tackling a ball carrier who's intending to throw a forward pass; forcing a fumble; or forcing a ball carrier out of bounds, behind the line of scrimmage on an intended pass play.

safety — A player position on defense. (See "free safety" and "strong safety"). Also a method of scoring (two points) by downing an opposing ball carrier in his own end zone, or if the offensive team commits a foul while in its own end zone, most notably intentional grounding.

safety valve — A receiver, often a running back, whose job it is to get open for a short pass in case all other primary receivers are covered.

Sam — The strong side outside linebacker, usually aligned over a tight end. Could be any name beginning with an "s" for "strong."

scat back — A running back who is quick, fast and good at juking around defenders as opposed to running them over like a "power" back.

scoop and score — A fumble recovered by the defense that results in a touchdown.

scout team — During practices, the team that emulates the offensive plays and defensive sets of the opponent based on scouting reports. The purpose is to help familiarize themselves with what to expect from the opposition come game time.

scramble or quarterback scramble — On a passing play, when the quarterback leaves the pocket to avoid being sacked, giving the receivers more time to get open or attempting to gain yards by running himself.

screen pass — A short forward pass to a receiver behind the line of scrimmage to a player who, if the play is executed properly, will have a couple of blockers in front of him. The receiver is usually a running back, although wide receiver and tight end screens are also used.

scrimmage — An informal practice matchup, either between two teams or between different units of the same team, under game conditions, or particular situations such as short yardage, long yardage or goal line situations.

secondary — Label for the defensive "backfield," specifically the safeties and cornerbacks. Primarily responsible for pass coverage followed by run defense.

shield punt — A punting formation with seven players on the line of scrimmage and three others 7 to 10 yards deep to protect the punter behind them.

shift — When one or more offensive players move to a different position at the same time before the snap. All players who move in a shift must come to a complete one-second stop prior to the snap.

shooting — The action of a linebacker or defensive back to blitz, attempting to "shoot the gap" between offensive blockers.

shotgun formation — Offensive alignment in which the team lines up with the quarterback receiving the snap 5-8 yards behind the center instead of directly behind the center.

sideline —The lines marking the out-of-bounds areas on each side of the field.

simulating the (snap) count — An infraction whereby the defensive team illegally calls out an imitation of the snap count in order to disrupt the offensive team and make the opposition "jump the gun." 5-yard penalty.

single wing — Formations, highly popular between 1906 and World War II, that typically used an unbalanced line, shotgun snap, and one wingback to produce a power-running offense that utilized fakery in ball handling in the backfield.

slant — A pass-receiving route in which a receiver runs straight up field a few yards, plants his outside foot hard while in full stride, and turns 45 degrees to the inside.

slobber-knocker — A particularly gruesome tackle or hit, usually eliciting loud accolades at team film sessions.

slot — The area between a split end and the rest of the offensive line. A pass receiver lined up between the split end and offensive tackle is called a slot back receiver.

slow play — A technique by which a defender, against an option offense, tries to delay the quarterback's decision by not showing him a quick reaction, so more of his mates can pursue and help make the play on the ball carrier.

smash mouth — Term for physical, straight-ahead running offense, aimed at running over the defense rather than tricking or out running it.

snap — The handoff or pass from the center that begins a play from scrimmage.

snap count — The "hut" sound the quarterback will use to signal for the snap to be made. It can be a word, number, or in a shotgun formation, a signal that the center can see.

sneak — An offensive play in which the quarterback, receiving the snap from directly behind the center, plows forward with the ball when a team needs a short gain for a first down or touchdown.

spearing — The act of a player illegally using his helmet to lead in contacting an opponent, resulting in a 15-yard penalty — and, under targeting rules, may lead to his being ejected from the game.

special teams — The units that handle kickoffs, punts, free kicks and field goal attempts. On kicking plays, also termed "suicide squads" because of the sometimes-vicious hits that occur.

spike — A play in which the quarterback throws the ball at the ground immediately after the snap to stop the clock. Technically an incomplete pass, it is not considered intentional grounding.

splits — The distance between the feet of adjacent offensive linemen. Wide splits, if there's a large gap between players (more than three feet), or narrow splits, if the gap is small (less than two feet).

split end — A receiver, "X," who lines up on the line of scrimmage, several yards outside the interior offensive linemen.

spot — The location determined by the official where the ball was downed or blown dead.

spy — A defender who is assigned to cover the quarterback, no matter where he goes. Used against elusive quarterbacks dropping back to pass.

squib kick — A type of kickoff in which the ball is intentionally kicked low to the ground to prevent a long return. Typically, the ball bounces on the ground a few times before being picked up by one of the blockers instead of the designated kickoff returner.

starter — A player who begins ("first string") at a particular position as the game or season gets underway.

Statue of Liberty — Trick play in which the quarterback, looking one way, raises the ball as if to pass and, instead, gives it to a player running laterally behind him.

sticks — The two poles attached to the end of the 10-yard chain used to measure for a new series of downs — i.e., the line to gain a new "first down."

stiff-arm or straight-arm — The act of a ball carrier pushing away would-be tacklers with a straight arm.

stretching the defense — Offensive formations and plays designed to force the defense to widen and defend the entire width of the field for each play.

strip — To separate a football from the player carrying it.

strong safety (SS) — A position on defense whose responsibilities are opposed to those of the free safety. A strong safety lines up on the strong side of the formation to the tight end side, defending the run first and pass second.

strong side — The side of the formation on which the tight end is aligned or has the most offensive players. Defensive coaches may have their own individual method of determining the strong side of an offensive formation.

stuff — A hard, physical tackle of a ball carrier on a running play behind the line of scrimmage, comparable to a sack on a pass play but not with an accompanying statistical category.

stunt — A tactic used by defensive linemen in which they switch responsibilities on the snap of the ball in an attempt to confuse, and get past, the blockers.

sweep — A running play in which several blockers lead a running back on a designed play to the outside of the offensive formation.

T

T formation — A classic offensive formation with the quarterback directly behind the center and three running backs behind and flanking the quarterback, forming a "T." Most often used in short-yardage situations where an extra blocking back might be helpful.

tackle — The act of the defense stopping and forcing a ball carrier to the ground. Also, a player position on the line, either an offensive tackle (OT) or a defensive tackle (DT).

tackle box — The area between where the two offensive tackles line up on the line of scrimmage prior to the snap.

tackle-eligible — A lineman who lines himself up in the position of an eligible receiver, as the end man of a seven-man unbalanced line, on the line of scrimmage. Defenses sometimes overlook such a player as a pass receiver because they're used to him only blocking.

tailback (TB) — Player position on offense who is the deepest running back, except in kicking formations. Also referred to as a running back, particularly in a one-back offense.

three-and-out — When an offensive team fails to gain a first down on the first three plays of a drive, and is forced to punt on fourth.

three-point stance — A down lineman's stance with three points on the ground: his two feet and one of his hands.

throwaway — To avoid being tackled for a loss, a quarterback's pass intentionally thrown in the vicinity of a receiver, but out of bounds with no chance of the pass being caught by an eligible receiver or defender.

tight end (TE) — A versatile player position on offense — a combination of an offensive lineman and receiver — who lines up on the line of scrimmage, next to the offensive tackle, and who does lots of blocking and a little pass-catching.

time of possession (TOP) — A statistic comprised of the amount of time one team has the ball in its offensive possession.

total offense — A statistic that combines yards rushing and yards passing.

touchback — The act of downing the ball behind one's own goal line on a kickoff or punt after the ball had been kicked over the goal line by the opposing team.

touchdown — A scoring play worth six points by having, or gaining, legal possession of the ball in the opponent's end zone or by the ball crossing the plane of the opponent's goal line with legal possession by a player.

trap — A basic blocking pattern in which a defensive lineman is allowed past the line of scrimmage, only to be surprised by a block at an angle by a "pulling" lineman out of his eyesight.

trenches — The battleground along the line of scrimmage and three yards deep where the offensive and defensive linemen mix it up every play of the football game.

trick play — Any of a variety of plays that use deception to catch the other team off-guard. Also known as "gadget play."

trips — A formation in which three wide receivers are lined up on the same side of the field, with one on the line of scrimmage and the others one yard off the ball. Short for "triple."

true freshman — A player who is one year out of high school, contrasting with a redshirt freshman who has practiced with the team for one year while attending college, but who has not yet played in a game.

try — A try is awarded to a team that has just scored a touchdown. The try allows the offense to score an additional one point on a successful kick or two points on a successful pass or run. Also called "try-for-point," "conversion," "extra point(s)," "point(s) after (touchdown)" or "PAT."

turnover on downs — When a team uses all four of its downs without scoring or making a first down, it must relinquish the ball to the other team.

turnover — The loss of the ball by one team to the other team, usually as a result of a fumble, an interception or turnover by downs.

two-point conversion — After a touchdown, a play from the 3-yard-line (college) and 2-yard-line (pros) worth two points if the offense can score via run or pass.

U

unbalanced line — An offensive formation that does not have an equal number of linemen on each side of the ball, intended to gain a blocking advantage on one side of the formation. A common alignment would be End-Guard-Center-Guard-Tackle-Tackle-End.

under center — The quarterback lining up directly behind the center to take a hand off snap. The person under center is considered ineligible to catch a pass in the NFL, but is an eligible receiver in college and high school.

up back — A player, in a kick from scrimmage — punts and field goals — who lines up behind the offensive line to block oncoming defensive players.

up man — During a kickoff, every player on the return team is called an "up man" with the exception of the one or two designated kickoff returners. All players on the return team are eligible to call for a fair catch.

utility player — A player capable of playing multiple positions.

V

vanilla offense/defense — An offense with very few plays and/or formations (boring). Used when coaches don't want to reveal much of their schemes to upcoming opponents.

victory formation — In the final seconds of a game, an offensive play where the quarterback of the team with the lead receives the snap and kneels, killing the play, but allowing the clock to run out.

veer —A type of option offense where the offensive tackle and guard may angle-lock towards the center, leaving a defensive lineman unblocked. If the unblocked defender tackles the running back going to that hole, the quarterback keeps the ball and then options off the next defender outside.

W

walk-on — In college, a player who is not receiving a scholarship but has earned a spot on the team.

wall — On a kickoff or punt, when players on the return team peel off toward the sideline while the ball is in the air. They position themselves a few yards apart, facing inside to create a line of blockers who don't have a particular man to go after, but block any defender in their area.

weak side — The true side of the formation opposite the tight end. It may also be the side of the field with the fewest offensive players.

West Coast Offense — An offensive philosophy using short, high-percentage passes as the focus of a ball-control offense. Originally made popular by San Francisco 49ers coach Bill Walsh, it is widely used. The offense emphasizes short routes for receivers and using short passes to replace runs. It relies heavily on yardage from running after the catch, using many eligible receivers on plays to maximize quarterback options, and spreading the ball to many targets to keep the defense confused.

wheel route — A pass route in which a receiver or running back runs parallel to the line of scrimmage towards the sideline and then takes off up the field to isolate a faster receiver against a slower linebacker or safety.

wide — Adjective meaning "towards the sidelines." Example: A kick that is "wide left" has missed to the left of the goal posts.

wide receiver (WR) — An offensive receiver split wide (usually about 10 yards) from the formation who plays on the line of scrimmage as a split end, "X," or 1 yard off as a flanker, "Z."

wildcat offense — An offensive formation in which a running back replaces the quarterback and receives a direct snap from center and runs a predetermined play.

Will — The weakside linebacker, aligning opposite the offense's tight end. Could be any name beginning with a "w" for "weak."

wingback (WB) — A player position, lining up just outside the tight end one yard off the line of scrimmage in position to be used as a receiver, blocker and/or runner of reverses and counter plays.

wishbone — An offensive formation involving three running backs lined up behind the quarterback in the shape of a Y, similar to the shape of a wishbone. Rare these days.

X

x's and o's — Symbols used in football diagrams: the x's are defensive and the o's offensive players.

X-receiver — The split end or the wide receiver who lines up on the line of scrimmage outside the offensive tackle to his side.

Y

YAC — Yards After Catch, or the distance the ball carrier ran after the catch. Also: Yards After Contact, which is the amount of yardage gained by a runner after the first tackler contacts him.

Y-receiver — The offense's primary tight end in a play.

yard line — A marking on the field indicating the distance, in yards, to the nearest goal line.

yardage — The amount of yards gained or lost during a play, game, season or career.

yards from scrimmage — The amount of yards gained by the offensive team advancing the ball from the line of scrimmage.

Z

Z-receiver — Used in offensive play-calling to refer to the flanker — the wide receiver who lines up at least a yard behind the line of scrimmage.

zebra — A colloquial term, not always used with affection, for an official that refers to his black-and-white striped uniform.

zone defense — A defense in which players are responsible for pass-coverage areas of the field instead of covering individual receivers.

zone blitz — A defensive package combining a blitz — five or more rushers — with zone-pass coverage.

zone read — An option offense with the quarterback and running back lined up side-by-side. Reading the defensive reaction to putting the ball into the belly of the running back, the quarterback either completes the handoff or keeps it and runs it himself.

Bibliography

Football, issued by the Aviation Training Division, U.S. Naval Institute, Annapolis, Maryland, 1943.

Hill, Dean. *Football Thru the Years*. New York: Gridiron Publishing Company, Georgian Press, 1940.

Johnston, Daryl. *Watching Football, Discovering the Game Within the Game*. Guilford, Connecticut: The Globe Pequot Press, 2005.

Layden, Tim. *Blood, Sweat and Chalk*. New York: Time Home Entertainment, Inc., 2010.

Leahy, Frank. *Notre Dame Football: The T Formation*. New York: Prentice-Hall Inc., 1949.

Murphy, Austin. *Saturday Rules*. New York: Harper Collins Publishers, 2007.

Oriard, Michael. *How the Popular Press Created an American Spectacle*. Chapel Hill, North Carolina: University of North Carolina Press, 1993.

Acknowledgments

Thanks for the inspiration of Roscoe Divine, who, for several years, encouraged me to write this book and then put his financial support behind the project.

Frank Landrum, Kipp Preble, Don and Karen Harney, Curtis Anderson and Jim Chapman lent their editorial feedback to the project. Jeff Lyford lent his vast technical experience to the development of my domain and website.

I also owe a great debt of gratitude to Jerry Thompson, editor of *Mighty Oregon* magazine, who contributed his excellent game photographs to accent points in the book; the Monday night's "Not Dead Yet Poet's Society," which provided nearly always-positive encouragement for the venture; and the ongoing film studies and analysis with accomplished football coaches led by my Best Man, Denny Schuler, an incredible football mind who has been fired more times than a Gatling Gun.

I have been gifted to have worked with outstanding coaches who were also great men: Don Harney, Jerry Frei, John Robinson, Bruce Snyder, Norm Chapman, George Seifert, Ron Stratten, Jim Owens, Jim Walden and countless others, who so loved the game they thought nothing of spending time talking and teaching it to an eager young coach.

To all my players —Ducks, Huskies, Missionaries, Aggies, Cougars and Bears — and to all my viewers and readers: thank you for your patience and for allowing me to share my love of football with you. It's such an awesome game. You can learn so much, suffer so much and have so much fun — all at the same time.

Made in the USA
Lexington, KY
03 December 2018